ERNÖ GOLDFINGER

ERNÖ GOLDFINGER

ROBERT ELWALL

A.D. ACADEMY EDITIONS

ACKNOWLEDGEMENTS

Published in collaboration with the Royal Institute of British Architects.
All illustrative material is from the British Architectural Library, Drawings and Photographs Collections,
Royal Institute of British Architects.

SERIES EDITOR: Jill Lever
From an original idea by Stuart Durant

FRONT COVER: Competition design for a shopping centre at the Elephant and Castle, London,
for Imry Properties Ltd, 1960 (see plate no. 64)
BACK COVER: Design for alterations to 13 West Hill, Highgate, London,
for Andrew Wordsworth, 1939 (see plate no. 34)
PAGE 2: Ernö Goldfinger at Balfron Tower, Rowlett Street estate, London
(photo: Sam Lambert, 1968)

Published in Great Britain in 1996 by
ACADEMY EDITIONS
an imprint of

ACADEMY GROUP LTD
42 Leinster Gardens, London W2 3AN
Member of VCH PUBLISHING GROUP

ISBN: 1 85490 444 2

Distributed to the trade in the USA by
NATIONAL BOOK NETWORK, INC
4720 Boston Way, Lanham, Maryland 20706

Printed and bound in Singapore

CONTENTS

FOREWORD

The RIBA's single largest and most comprehensive collection is of Ernö Goldfinger's drawings, models and manuscripts – virtually all of his surviving works on paper as well as his office documentation. In 1963, following the publication of a special issue of *Architectural Design* on Goldfinger the RIBA Librarian, James Palmes, wrote to the architect asking for 'one or two' drawings. Goldfinger's reply was, 'I am flattered that you should want . . . my drawings . . . I have got thousands and would be glad to get rid of some of them'. Quite a large number came in 1972, followed by the bulk of the drawings in 1976, though a trickle continued to arrive until 1989. The manuscript material – job correspondence files, other correspondence, office diaries, off-prints, etc – came between 1977 and 1993. In all there are about 12,000 drawings and 75,000 office papers, as well as nineteen models and such things as samples of Goldfinger-designed door furniture and the nameplate to his office.

The earlier deposits of drawings and papers were presented on indefinite loan but this was eventually turned into a purchase, although the Library Committee was against paying for a living architect's work. Careful negotiation and good understanding, however, secured the collection for the RIBA, and at a fair price. Until his death in November 1987, Ernö Goldfinger, with his wife, Ursula, regularly visited the Drawings Collection to spend an hour or two putting the drawings in order, weeding out duplicate prints and the like, with Ernö occasionally adding (it is thought) his signature to some of the drawings. He enjoyed seeing his models displayed in the study rooms and his furniture drawings reproduced in a Drawings Collection publication and claimed that we had 'rediscovered' him.

Ernö Goldfinger's work is an essential part of British Modernism and an examination of it through his drawings is timely. I am grateful to Robert Elwall, my colleague at the RIBA for many years, for undertaking the third of a new series of monographs from the Drawings Collection of the Royal Institute of British Architects.

Jill Lever
(Series Editor of the RIBA Drawings Monographs)

PREFACE

The recent acquisition by the National Trust of 2 Willow Road, its first Modernist property, has turned the spotlight once again on the house's architect and former owner, Ernö Goldfinger. Goldfinger's architecture has always aroused strong feelings and since his death in 1987 his reputation generally has waned to the extent that one critic could splenetically remark that 'he is already languishing in Lethe's vale, deservedly forgotten, his name not to be found in current works of reference'. The story of Willow Road, however, provides a salient reminder that it is dangerous to dismiss the unfashionable. What outraged preservationists in the 1930s has now itself achieved heritage status. Similarly historians have begun to look afresh at the architectural legacy of the post-war years, a process of reassessment to which Goldfinger's career is crucial as it was then that his creative output was at its peak. Although the raw material exists, in the form of many thousands of drawings, letters and other office documents now preserved in the British Architectural Library, for a more detailed treatment, a study such as this can do no more than attempt to provide an introduction to a large body of work which was at once varied in scope and remarkably consistent in outlook.

As will be apparent several of the drawings reproduced are not in Goldfinger's own hand. It was often his practice to express his design ideas through informal sketches which would then be worked up into more formal drawings by assistants working under his close supervision. John Winter, who had two periods in Goldfinger's office in 1956 and 1959-60, recalled that Goldfinger liked to draw freehand in 3B pencil on butcher's paper and that 'you were expected to know all his work, and interpret his sketches accordingly'. 'Ernö himself draws very nicely but of all the drawings which came out of the office in my time then I can only think of two that were his. He worked through other people: when I first went there, there were only two of us working in the office, Denise Scott-Brown and myself. Even with funny people like us doing the drawings the buildings still came out the same way as genuine Goldfinger jobs'. Where possible drawings have been individually attributed. Where no attribution is given the drawing is either by Goldfinger or by an unknown hand.

Anyone writing about Goldfinger owes an enormous debt to James Dunnett who has tirelessly campaigned for greater recognition of his work. He has been generous with advice and help. I would also like to thank Jill Lever for inviting me to write the book and for her continuing support throughout; Angela Mace whose efforts over a prolonged period made Goldfinger's archive at the British Architectural Library as complete and fascinating as it is; Jane Collings and Andrea Meyer-Ludowisy who have with patience and skill undertaken the daunting task of sorting the papers into a comprehensible whole; Maggie Toy, Andrea and Mario Bettella, Rachel Bean and Steve Roberts at Academy; Sian Williams formerly of the British Architectural Library Drawings Collection; and AC Cooper Ltd who have done the photography. My largest debt of gratitude, however, is as always to my wife, Cathy, without whose unflagging efforts this book would not have been realised.

Sitting room, 2 Willow Road, London (photo: Sydney W Newbery, 1940)

INTRODUCTION

In 1963, with the first blocks of Alexander Fleming House nearing completion, *Architectural Design* devoted a special issue to the work of its architect, Ernö Goldfinger, with an introduction by Sir Herbert Read in which he maintained: 'The contribution which he [Goldfinger] has made to our architecture is one of the most distinctive of our time'.[1] Although thirty years later Goldfinger's place in the pantheon of British architects may seem less assured his work cannot easily be dismissed. His long career, which began against the backdrop of the Exposition Internationale des Arts Décoratifs, Paris (1925) and only ended with his retirement in 1977 as Piano & Rogers's high-tech Centre Pompidou opened, provides a unique opportunity to trace the development of Modernism in England. While many of the other émigré architects who found their way to British shores in the 1930s, such as Walter Gropius, Serge Chermayeff and Marcel Breuer, soon departed, Goldfinger stayed; while many of his 1930s MARS Group colleagues like Berthold Lubetkin and Wells Coates produced their best work before the war but little after it, Goldfinger's career only reached maturity in the late 1950s and 1960s. Though Goldfinger often seems to have ploughed a lonely furrow, his work does in fact encapsulate many of the key issues of its time, whether it be the struggle to establish Modernism in England in the 1930s, the subsequent battle for its soul in the 1950s, or the impassioned debate engendered by high-rise housing a decade later. Even after his death it has still continued to excite controversy. The future of Alexander Fleming House has been central to considerations of what should be preserved and what the criteria for listing buildings should be. Austere and rational, at times menacing, oblivious to changing styles, Goldfinger's work occupies a unique, if not altogether popular, place in British twentieth-century architecture.

Goldfinger's approach to architectural design was forged in the heady atmosphere of artistic revolt and experimentation prevailing in Paris in the 1920s. Born in Budapest in 1902, Goldfinger was the son of a Vienna lawyer who had been sent to manage the family estates and sawmills in Transylvania. In 1919 after the collapse of the Austro-Hungarian empire the Goldfingers moved to Vienna and Ernö was subsequently sent to Le Rosay School in Gstaad, Switzerland, and finally to Paris in 1920 to complete his education. Inspired as a boy by his mother's copy of Hermann Muthesius's *Das englische Haus* (1904-05) and by the colourful drawings of the architect his parents had hired to convert one of their houses, Goldfinger abandoned plans to become a sculptor and instead chose to study architecture. After two years in the atelier of Léon Jaussely, Professor of Archaeology, he gained admittance to the prestigious Ecole Nationale Supérieure des Beaux-Arts in 1923. During his fourteen years in Paris Goldfinger met and became friends with many leading avant-garde artists including Ernst, Man Ray and Ozenfant, whose work he collected and later hung at Willow Road. He was also a member of the group which gathered regularly at the fashionable Café du Dôme and it was here that he encountered the Austrian Modernist architect, Adolf Loos, who was to be a major influence on his designs for interiors later in the decade. Goldfinger also first met an even more influential figure at this time, Le Corbusier, whom he interviewed for a Hungarian newspaper after the publication of his seminal *Vers une architecture* in 1923 which Goldfinger described as 'a terrific revelation for me'.[2] This artistic ferment and the revolutionary changes that were sweeping through European architecture were not, however, reflected in the teaching at the Ecole and Goldfinger became increasingly frustrated by its innate conservatism. He later recalled: 'At the Beaux Arts everything was dead. All the stirring of modern architecture was ridiculed. The pompous projects for subjects like a "Governor's Palace in Annam" or a "French Embassy in Central America", were just so many exercises in the application of the orders. In the country of the *Galeries des Machines* and of Labrouste, steel or reinforced concrete structures were simply ignored. We felt that something had to be done.'[3] As a result Goldfinger and a number of other dissatisfied students asked Le Corbusier to found a new atelier but he refused, suggesting instead his former employer, Auguste Perret. In 1925 the new atelier was duly established in a wing of Perret's Palais de Bois near the Porte Maillot.

Perret's reputation as the pioneer of reinforced concrete construction had recently been secured by the completion of Notre-Dame, Le Raincy (1924) and the influence he was to have on his new pupil would be hard to exaggerate. From Perret Goldfinger imbibed the ideas for reinforced concrete used in a strictly trabeated, classical manner and the frank expression of its structural frame that he was to explore over the next fifty years. Fond of aphorisms, Perret expressed one of his most cherished beliefs by declaring: 'He who hides any part of the framework deprives himself of the only legitimate and most beautiful ornament of architecture. He who hides a pillar makes a mistake. He who erects a false pillar commits a crime.'[4] This was to be a guiding principle of Goldfinger's own work as was Perret's deliberate courting of the 'banal' and avoidance of theatricality. Unlike Lubetkin, for example, who took obvious delight in the sculptural plasticity of concrete, Goldfinger's use of the material was rigorously disciplined, its effect reliant on the harmony of its proportions and its finish. Whereas, however, the mature work of some of Perret's pupils amounted to little more than sterile copyism, Goldfinger sought to marry Perret's constructional methods to the demands of the Modern Movement and, with the infusion of elements derived from other sources, successfully developed a distinctive style of his own.

Although highly respected, Perret was shunned by influential members of the architectural establishment who refused to forgive him for having left the Ecole without obtaining his diploma and disapproved of his involvement in his family's contracting business. Few of the projects submitted by his pupils were consequently accepted by the Beaux-Arts jury, a situation exacerbated by the jury's refusal to countenance reinforced concrete as a suitable material for the monumental architecture projects it set. This fact helps to explain Goldfinger's defensive remarks to the competition assessors for the Palace of Justice, San Salvador (1927) that 'this economic and rational mode of construction is absolutely not contrary to great monumental architecture'.[5] Confronted by such hostility Goldfinger left Perret's atelier in 1926 and joined that of the conservative Alphonse Alexandre Defrasse, finally achieving his diploma in 1932.

Although Perret's was the prime influence on Goldfinger, his was by no means the only one. As Goldfinger's early drawings reveal, the Beaux-Arts for all its shortcomings not only afforded him a thorough training in the techniques of sound construction and taught him the importance of clarity in planning, it also introduced him to the new 'science' of town planning, Perret's neglect of which Le Corbusier had criticised. Goldfinger's first *chef d'atelier*, Jaussely, who was instrumental in having Raymond Unwin's writings translated into French, taught the subject to his pupils and Goldfinger subsequently attended classes in *urbanisme* at the Sorbonne from 1926 to 1928. These studies bore fruit firstly in a number of town planning projects undertaken in the late 1920s and early 1930s, such as those for Philippeville, Angers and Antwerp, as well as the CIAM housing scheme of 1933; then later in his publication, the *County of London Plan Explained* (1943); and finally in his proposals for the redevelopment of the Elephant and Castle. This concern to see architecture in the wider context of urban planning, alien to many British architects but typical of the Modern Movement, informed all of Goldfinger's work even though he was denied the opportunity to put his ideas fully into effect.

While studying at the Ecole Goldfinger also set up in practice with a fellow Hungarian, András Szivessy (1901-58), who later changed his name to André Sive and played a key role in the reconstruction of post-war France as well as being one of the only two European architects invited to be competition assessors for the town plan of Brasilia. Most of the work of the partnership until its dissolution in 1930, and Goldfinger's on his own account in Paris thereafter, consisted of furniture and shop designs and the remodelling of apartment interiors for a string of well-heeled and bohemian clients such as Suzanne Blum and the artist, Richard Wyndham. Unfortunately relatively few drawings of these schemes survive, but to judge from existing photographs the most noteworthy were the Central European Express Travel Bureau, Paris (1927) and the Helena Rubinstein salon in London of the same date (see p12). Some of these interiors were characterised by their austerity, walls lined with plywood being a predominant feature; in others, new materials such as Bakelite were used with chrome and steel to create an illusion of sumptuousness. A desire to experiment with indirect lighting effects was also very evident. These interior designs owed much to the work of Loos, in particular two contemporary commissions in Paris, the house for Tristan Tzara (1927) and the ornate Knizé Gentlemen's Outfitters on the Champs-Elysées (1927), both of which Goldfinger knew and admired. The contrast often to be found in Goldfinger's later work between hard-edged,

pared-down exteriors and more richly embellished interiors, such as the marble-clad entrance hall of Trellick Tower (1972), for example, can perhaps be traced to the dual legacy of Perret and Loos.

Goldfinger's Parisian years left an indelible impression on him. When he moved to London in 1934 with his English wife, Ursula Blackwell, whom he had married the previous year, Goldfinger's architectural training, with its emphasis on geometry, logic and urbanism, set him apart from the majority of his new English colleagues for whom the tradition of the picturesque, stressing the relationship of the building to its setting, remained pre-eminent. Few British architects had trained at the Beaux-Arts and for all his criticisms of it Goldfinger felt justified in maintaining that his education was far superior to the ill-defined empiricism to be found in English architectural schools. This sense of isolation was intensified by his difficulty in finding work, a problem shared by other Modernist architects. Unlike Oliver Hill who was prepared to try his hand at any style and with whom Goldfinger became firm friends after the Paris Exhibition of 1937, Goldfinger refused to compromise his principles, telling the *Daily Sketch*'s reporter, 'I could make lots more money if I designed neo-Tudor or Georgian abominations but I won't'.[6] Although this stance was no doubt aided by his relative financial security – his wife's family was part of the Crosse & Blackwell food empire – it was also typical of a career which was marked by its integrity and honesty of outlook.

Goldfinger's pre-war work in England was thus restricted to the sort of commissions which he had previously undertaken in Paris – shops, interiors, furniture, the occasional small house, and an increasing number of exhibition stands. His main clients during this period were Paul and Marjorie Abbatt, the innovative toy-makers, for whom Goldfinger designed a range of toys; their new shop in Wimpole Street (1936) – one of the finest of the inter-war years (see p12); exhibition displays at Dorland

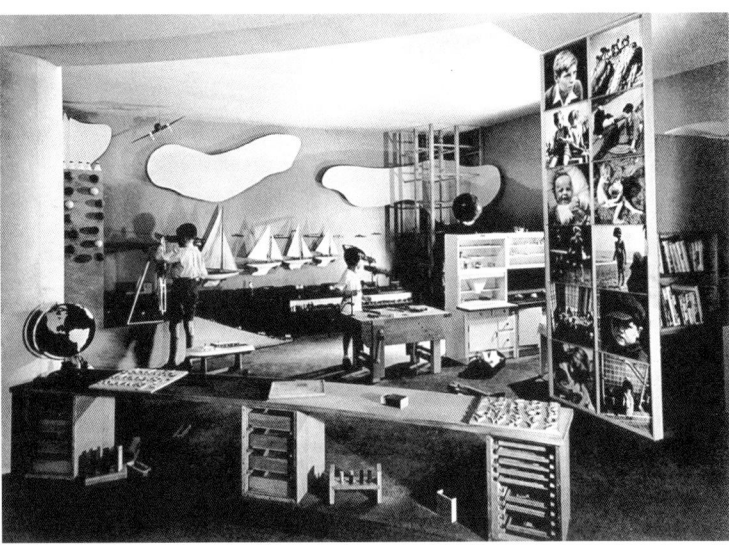

FROM ABOVE, L TO R: Central European Express, Paris (photo: Marius Gravot, from Roger Poulain's Boutiques *(Paris, 1929)); Helena Rubinstein salon, London (photo: Bryan Westwood, 1937); Abbatt shop, London (1937); children's section, British Pavilion, Paris (photo: Millar & Harris, 1937)*

Hall (1934) and Paris (1937) (see p12); and their flat in Tavistock Square (1936). Indeed designing for children was to be a key theme of Goldfinger's work at this time and of particular note is a series of interesting designs for low-cost prefabricated schools which were unassuming precursors of the much-admired post-war school building programme. An intimation of later work was his involvement with the estate agent-cum-developer, PH Edwards, in a project to transform Seaford, on the Sussex coast, into a seaside development similar to that being attempted contemporaneously by Oliver Hill at Frinton. The project was eventually abandoned with little built but not before Goldfinger had written to Frank Lloyd Wright in 1935 requesting copies of his drawings for Broadacre City which he believed 'was designed for a community of this sort and I should be interested to see your interpretation of it'.[7] Apparently Wright did not reply.

Without doubt the most significant of Goldfinger's pre-war works was the block of three brick-faced houses at 1-3 Willow Road, Hampstead, completed in 1939. The controversy surrounding the houses, the central one of which Goldfinger designed for his own use, was in large measure based on their opponents' mistaken belief that they were to be Corbusian, flat-roofed, white, concrete boxes of the type erected by Connell Ward & Lucas in nearby Frognal in 1938. In fact Goldfinger was never beguiled by the refulgently photogenic, siren forms of continental Modernism, declaring: 'I want to be remembered as a Classical architect, not a kasbah architect'.[8] Willow Road thus firmly belongs to that last phase of pre-war British Modernism when doctrinal insistence on the use of reinforced concrete and white walls was giving way to a wider appreciation of other materials such as wood and brick.[9] This change can be seen in houses at Tewin by Mary Crowley (1936) and at Halland by Serge Chermayeff (1938), as well as in a house by Samuel & Harding in nearby Arkwright Road (1938) to which Goldfinger's terrace bears some similarities. Unlike Patrick Gwynne's Homewood, Esher (1939) – also destined to become National Trust property – which looked abroad for its inspiration, Willow Road drew mainly upon indigenous sources. In common with many other Modernist architects, Goldfinger greatly admired Georgian architecture, the harmony and beauty of its proportions having first been drawn to his attention by another enthusiast, Adolf Loos. Willow Road was Goldfinger's reinterpretation of the Georgian terrace and an interesting attempt, following on from that of Lubetkin & Pilichowski at Genesta Road, Plumstead (1934), to revive the terrace as an acceptable urban form and as a much-needed antidote to the wave of semi-detached houses threatening to engulf London. The scheme was thus very much in keeping with Goldfinger's notions of town planning which stressed the importance of the neighbourhood in forging social cohesion.

The Willow Road controversy, whilst obviously less bitter than earlier confrontations such as the *Listener* debates 'For and Against Modern Architecture' (1934) or the distasteful episode of the Bexhill Pavilion (1934) with its outpouring of anti-Semitic bile, nevertheless demonstrates how far from public acceptance, even in a supposedly enlightened area like Hampstead, modern architecture remained at the end of the decade for all the propagandising of *The Architectural Review* and the seductive images of its photographers, Dell & Wainwright. By showing, however, that modern architecture was not simply 'kasbah' architecture, Willow Road played a small part in making it publicly acceptable. After the war its example was adopted, albeit in diluted form, by Frederick Gibberd at Harlow and its stock progressively rose. In 1955 Goldfinger's house was revisited by *House and Garden* in an article significantly entitled 'Still Ahead of Its Time'[10] and in 1970 it was listed. Two years later Christopher Gotch, decrying the fact that the National Trust owned no post-Georgian buildings of any architectural significance, called for this omission to be remedied by the acquisition of

Willow Road,[11] and over twenty years later this has finally come to pass. Whilst it is ironic that 2 Willow Road is now to be preserved by the National Trust, the very guardian of those picturesque principles which Goldfinger frequently berated for their romantic sentimentality, it is striking testament to a house that has worn so much better and looks less obviously of its period than its superficially more glamorous contemporaries. The house has triumphantly vindicated Henry-Russell Hitchcock's prescient observation made in 1937 that 'although modern buildings with brick, tile or stone surfaces will at first be less effective as propaganda than those covered with light-coloured rendering, they will probably grow old more gracefully'.[12]

In retrospect Willow Road can be seen not as an elegiac farewell to the 1930s but as an anticipation of the eagerly awaited New Jerusalem to come. Far from snuffing out the Modern Movement, the war helped to ensure its eventual triumph. As the *Architects' Journal* recognised in 1941: 'What World War I did to the aeroplane, World War 2 has done to modern architecture. It has turned it from a fad into a national necessity. War has cut the laziness, the clichés, the heavy-handed what-I've-always-done right out of architectural practice.'[13] By 1945, with devastated cities in urgent need of rebuilding, Modernism was the architectural equivalent of that year's Labour Party election victory – an expression of the desire for change and a determination not to return to the bad old days of Auden's 'devil's decade'. The spate of exhibitions and discussion forums held throughout the land in such unlikely settings as shops, restaurants, and canteens, which became a feature of cultural life in wartime Britain, helped to bring this transformation about. As a noncombatant Goldfinger played an active role in this winning over of public opinion, particularly through the series of exhibitions which he designed for the Army Bureau of Current Affairs (ABCA), the Admiralty, and the Air Ministry Directorate of Educational Services. Simply

and boldly presented, these exhibitions, such as the *LCC Plan for London* (1944), *Traffic* (1944), and *Planning Your Neighbourhood* (1945), mainly dealt with issues that would need to be addressed by post-war society. Goldfinger's left-of-centre views also saw his involvement in other exhibitions which tackled more pressing concerns, including *Twenty-five Years of Soviet Progress* held at the Wallace Collection in 1942 to bolster support for Russia, and the sale of modern art which he organised the following year at Willow Road to raise funds for the Red Army.

The war years offered an opportunity to take stock and to consider how post-war reconstruction could best be achieved. Goldfinger spent his time profitably in exploring ideas for post-war housing where the problem of rebuilding would be at its most acute. Of particular importance were the investigations into box-frame methods of construction which he carried out with Ove Arup: the system formulated during this period providing the basis for his large post-war housing projects. As air-raids increasingly took their toll it became obvious that the housing problem could not be tackled without recourse to prefabrication. Although Goldfinger had experimented with prefabricated systems before the war and was to do so again afterwards in an ingeniously devised but rather limited scheme employed to build primary schools at Brandlehow Road, Wandsworth, and Westville Road, Hammersmith, in 1950, he remained sceptical. The teamwork implied by prefabrication, the need for the architect to step down, as Lord Esher put it, 'from his Renaissance pedestal'[14] and to become an anonymous cog in a well oiled machine, did not appeal to an artist–architect like Goldfinger. Above all, however, Goldfinger believed in building for permanence. He abhorred the temporary and the *Builder* reported in 1943 that he felt: 'Prefabrication was only justified if it benefited the operative and consumer. He thought that the site factory was a rational way of dealing with large housing schemes. Regarding the life of the house, he thought it was a mistaken and uneconomic view that houses should be built on a short term policy; this would lead only to jerry-building methods and to "fashion" in houses as in cars.'[15] When in the 1960s Goldfinger designed his first high-rise housing schemes these were built using *in-situ* poured concrete and thus avoided many of the problems which plagued contemporary system-built blocks.

In 1946 Goldfinger became a British citizen and opened an office at 69-70 Piccadilly, but in the immediate aftermath of war there were few opportunities for the private architect. Licenses were required to build, the few available construction materials were directed to the priority areas of housing and schools, and most building was carried out under the auspices of the burgeoning local authority architects' departments staffed by a younger generation of architects returning from the front. The shortage of work even tempted some private architects like Max Fry and Jane Drew to pursue their careers in the colonies. For his part Goldfinger was forced to survive on a frugal diet of commissions, the most notable of which were the Communist Party headquarters, King Street, London (1946), and more importantly the *Daily Worker* building, Farringdon Road, London (1946), both executed in collaboration with the Communist, Colin Penn, with whom Goldfinger was briefly in partnership from 1946 to 1948. An indication of the scarcity of work in the private sector is provided by two intriguing applications for jobs which Goldfinger made in 1948 – one as assistant to Lubetkin at Peterlee (what a fiery combination those two would have made!) and the other as head of Stevenage Development Corporation.[16] When, in 1951, he was invited to make only a modest contribution of some kiosks to the Festival of Britain it seemed that Goldfinger's career might well fizzle out, as that of Wells Coates, another minor participant in the Festival, was shortly to do. This possibility was given added credence by the leading roles played in the Festival by two of Goldfinger's pre-war assistants, Ralph Tubbs and HT Cadbury-Brown. A new breed of architects seemed set to take over – Donald Gibson in Coventry, Frederick Gibberd in Harlow, for instance – giving permanent built form to the Festival's architectural ideals, ideals which were anathema to Goldfinger who was one of a growing throng disillusioned with what they regarded as their Swedish-inspired whimsicality. Yet within five years, when he was one of the leading architect participants in the significantly entitled *This Is Tomorrow* exhibition held at the Whitechapel Art Gallery in 1956, where he shared a platform with angry young architects like Alison and Peter Smithson, Goldfinger was about to embark on the most productive years of his career. This transformation was not merely due to the relaxation of building restrictions in 1954 but also to a radical change in architectural climate which saw the values he had consistently espoused come to the fore – a tougher, less sentimental approach to design; an emphasis on the frank expression of materials and in particular on concrete as the primary building material; and a willingness to experiment with high-rise. Underlying this shift was the perception that the Modern Movement needed to regain the visionary fervour and hard cutting edge of its 'heroic' period lost in the cosy populism of the Festival and the architecture of the expanding New Towns. To distinguish it from the New Empiricism or New Humanism of the Festival with its picturesque informality and eclectic choice of materials, this new uncompromising movement led by the Smithsons was dubbed New Brutalism. It looked not to Sweden for its inspiration but to those revered masters of the Modern Movement who were still practising, in particular Ludwig Mies van der Rohe and Le Corbusier, whose *béton brut* masterpiece, the Unité d'Habitation, Marseilles (1946-52) made a tremendous impact on British architects, not least on Goldfinger.

For a decade from the mid-1950s, therefore, Goldfinger found himself more in demand than at any previous stage in his career, engaged not just on small, private commissions but also on larger, more monumental projects for which his Beaux-Arts training had left him well prepared. In these works he was to evolve a mature style of his own, the logic and clarity of which did indeed evoke the revolutionary spirit of the Modern Movement's pioneering years. Designs were stripped down to their basic elements and in the same way as he had hoped Willow Road might become the prototype for a new form of urban terrace so prototypical solutions were devised for different building types, especially offices and high-rise housing. In 1963 Goldfinger reckoned: 'Looking back and statistically analysing what I have done over the past five years, I have come to the simple conclusion that all I have been building is big decks – platforms one on top of the other. I shall go on doing this until I find something better. When I build offices I build decks. When I build hospitals, schools, flats, even houses, I build decks. All of them are subdivided as you like by partitions and are enclosed by an outside skin which, if you like, you can also alter.'[17] The buildings of this period originated in a rational re-examination of first principles and, employing a narrow range of materials, played variations on a strictly limited theme. They also became, in the forms of Alexander Fleming House (see p20), Balfron Tower (1968) and Trellick Tower (see p20), increasingly overbearing in scale and intimidatingly oppressive in character – examples of the sublime expressed in Modern Movement terms.

A feature common to many of these works was Goldfinger's use of the 2-foot 9-inch planning grid which he had formulated to streamline production and standardise detailing. This grid had first been illustrated in the ABCA exhibition *Planning Your Home* (1946) and was first employed in designing the house for Colonel Fletcher at Henley-in-Arden in the following year. 'I am a very practical person', Goldfinger explained in 1963, 'I don't start off with theories. I see a problem; and I try to solve it. But in architecture, especially modern architecture where so many different building components have to be brought under some sort of control, discipline and analysis are very important. I base everything I do on the dimension two feet nine inches. I don't make a fetish about this. I use it because it is handy to me. Two feet nine is the width of the standard door and its jamb. Either way on a square, it is also the width of a man standing comfortably with his hands on his hips. Multiply this by four and I have a grid into which . . . I can fit my whole building.'[18] This scientific approach to architectural design was also reflected in Goldfinger's increasingly systematic application of the Golden Section, the Albemarle Street office building (1956) being the most obvious example (see p20). Goldfinger revealed: 'Since the late 1920s I have used the properties of rectangles which all resemble each other but have quite different properties. $1\sqrt{2}$; 2:3; and the Golden section 1:1•618 – looking at the building you cannot tell one from the other but when you build up the facade or the plan you mustn't mix them. They all have their different, and sometimes conflicting, qualities.'[19]

Goldfinger's prototypical office building originated in his spare design in rough concrete for Carr & Co at Shirley in 1955 (see p20) and was refined in a series of schemes over the next two years – the Moorgate skyscraper project, also of 1955, the offices at Albemarle Street, and the unexecuted design for 69-70 Piccadilly (1957). The solutions worked out there to the particular problems of office design culminated in the massive complex of Alexander Fleming House. It is instructive to compare the Albemarle Street scheme, a rare instance of infill in Goldfinger's work and one of his best designs, with Peter Moro's Hille showrooms built two doors along the street in 1963. Moro's work, though an elegant example, was symptomatic of the type of office building that became all too prevalent on the London scene, an essay in glass curtain walling derived ultimately from Mies van der Rohe's Seagram Building, New York (1958). Goldfinger rejected this approach entirely, dismissing curtain walling as 'buildings with masks like those stockings burglars use',[20] and demanding instead that 'it must always be possible to see, and feel, how a building is supported'.[21] The Moorgate skyscraper and to a lesser extent Albemarle Street followed this central tenet of structural rationalism and the bold expression of their reinforced concrete frames and the alternating projections and recessions of their facades were themes taken up at Alexander Fleming House. Speaking about office design in 1957 Goldfinger maintained that there were three components of modern architecture: 'the permanent structure; the much less permanent services and an even more fleeting component, the human requirements'.[22] At Alexander Fleming House, therefore, the internal design was made as flexible as possible to allow changing subdivisions and easy re-routing of services. 'This new concept of the permanent and fleeting, of the constant and changing', Goldfinger argued, 'must be given shape. This shape is our new architecture.'[23]

Alexander Fleming House also reflected other changes on the architectural scene, particularly the emergence of the property developer as a major force in reshaping the urban fabric. The London County Council favoured Goldfinger's design for his client, Arnold Lee of Imry Properties, not merely because of its architectural merit but also because it promised the best financial return. Earlier the Moorgate skyscraper project had been undertaken specifically to investigate the economic potential of tall buildings and Mason Pearson, the landlord at Albemarle Street, had praised Goldfinger for getting 'more letting space out of that site than anybody in England could have done'.[24] Goldfinger's extraordinary talents as a planner proved irresistible to developer clients anxious to maximise rentable space and profits. To those who criticised the seeming apostasy of a left-wing architect fuelling the property boom Goldfinger responded: 'The economics of buildings for whomever they are carried out is the ratio of enclosed space to useable [sic] space. This equation means for the developer so much money spent per cubic foot of building, so much money received per square foot of lettable space . . . Somebody should tell the self-styled "socially conscious" architects about the facts of life and jolt them out of their fairyland of make-believe.'[25] In truth Goldfinger never allowed politics to intrude into architecture and his work for Imry and other developers only served to underline the heterogeneous nature of his client group which also embraced avant-garde artists, the confidante of the Duchess of Windsor, social idealists like the Abbatts, the collective Peoples Printing Press and local authorities.

It was during the late 1950s that Goldfinger also further elaborated his ideas for high-rise housing in a scheme for Watford Rural District Council at Abbots Langley (1956). Drawing on designs by the Smithsons for Golden Lane in the City of London and by JL Womersley, Jack Lynn and Ivor Smith for the Park Hill estate in Sheffield, both published in the previous year,[26] Goldfinger introduced the concept of an enclosed access gallery on every third floor serving a two person flat on the same level and four person flats above and below. This was to be the basic organisational principle of his two large housing schemes for the Greater London Council. Throughout his life Goldfinger remained a staunch champion of housing people in tower blocks, an early example being the project for a 23-storey block which he submitted to the influential Congrès International d'Architecture Moderne of 1933. This design, by providing communal facilities, eliminated the need for individual domestic arrangements which he considered inefficient. Goldfinger's advocacy of high-rise stemmed from his theories of urbanism and in particular from his unwavering belief in the notion of the concentrated city. Rejecting the ideas of Garden City planners such as Raymond Unwin and Frederic Osborn which he believed led inexorably to further suburban sprawl, Goldfinger argued that the solution to the housing problem was to concentrate city dwellers in tall blocks situated in fairly close proximity to one another, thus allowing economies in infrastructure and shortening the distances between home and school and home and work. Above all, such high density, vertical concentration would free surrounding land, for, in the famous CIAM phrase, 'soleil, espace, verdure'. Goldfinger continued to promote these ideas vigorously over the years whether it be in the article he published in *Ideal Home* in September 1942 which contributed to the house versus flat debate of the time, or in an interview he gave to the *Sunday Times* in 1960 where he unveiled his vision of London as 'a park city: not . . . a garden city'. If Hyde Park were to be extended into Bayswater, the Green Belt drawn in, and a network of urban motorways constructed, then Goldfinger felt: 'In 10 years . . . London could be a beautiful skyscraper city, and the view from the river could be as it was in Wren's London, except that instead of churches you would have skyscrapers towering over the lower buildings.'[27]

By the time of this interview the housing shortage had become particularly acute and in response the government encouraged high-rise developments and the use of industrialised building systems. Goldfinger was at last given the opportunity to put his theories into practice in two estates for the Greater London Council, at Rowlett Street in Poplar and at Edenham Street in North Kensington. Although the original brief for the former, drawn up in 1960, called for the design of four blocks, Goldfinger, in keeping with his long held principles, instead amalgamated them into a single 27-storey slab block with a range of communal facilities and a detached service tower. This layout was further developed in more striking fashion at Edenham Street. Uncompromisingly aggressive in nature and seeming to provide more of a bastion against their surroundings than a sympathetic response to them, these blocks reveal little of the utopian spirit which infused Goldfinger's urbanistic theories. In Goldfinger's

defence it has to be said that the building of Rowlett Street in stages denied him the chance to develop a design suitable for the site as a whole and as commonly happened 'soleil, espace, verdure' were sacrificed to the economic reality of crowding as many dwellings onto the site as possible. By the time of their completion in 1968 and 1972 respectively these tower blocks, amongst the tallest in the country, were already out of date. In the wake of the Ronan Point disaster of 1967 popular opposition to such blocks could no longer be contained and in addition Darbourne & Darke's Lillington Gardens estate (1961-71) had shown that comparable densities could be achieved by more acceptable low-rise schemes. In contrast to Richard Seifert, however, whose public recantation of his support for high-rise housing Goldfinger had in mind when scornfully rebuking the 'drumming of breasts beaten in penance, by those responsible for some of the worst tall blocks',[28] Goldfinger steadfastly refused to concede that the concept itself was inherently flawed. Not without some justification he argued that the failure of high-rise lay rather in shoddy building techniques and poor management and maintenance. What can be said of Goldfinger's own blocks is that they were extraordinarily well built, meticulously detailed and generously planned. That is perhaps why they have proved generally popular with their residents.

The popular reaction against residential high-rise signalled the end of a career which through Goldfinger's long association with CIAM, his part in the foundation of the International Union of Architects, and his role as London correspondent of *l'Architecture d'aujourd'hui* from 1934 to 1974, injected a welcome spirit of cosmopolitanism into the often parochial British architectural scene. Goldfinger's influence has, however, been limited. Although the exacting standards he required of his staff ensured a high turnover, he never maintained a large office and seldom employed more than five or six assistants at any one time. Nor were lecturing or writing really his strengths despite the fine series of articles which he wrote for *The Architectural Review* in 1941-42.[29] Above all, his work, characterised by its rigorous pursuit of a narrow but consistent line of development based on the principles of structural rationalism, remained largely outside the mainstream of British architecture. Goldfinger was essentially an individualist who went his own way producing buildings that were soundly constructed, well proportioned and free of stylistic mannerisms. In the end it is hard to disagree with John Winter's verdict that 'small was often beautiful in his work'[30] and that Goldfinger is seen at his best in schemes such as Willow Road, Albemarle Street and the Wrightian Perry House (1968) where the striving for monumentality, evident in his later projects, is kept firmly in check.

Goldfinger has often been described as an architect's architect. Yet architecture is the most public of the arts and in some respects it could be said that his career epitomises the dangerous gap that has grown up between the profession and the public. It remains to be seen whether the acquisition of 2 Willow Road by the National Trust will be instrumental in widening appreciation of Goldfinger's work and whether this will eventually come to encompass larger schemes such as Alexander Fleming House and Trellick Tower or whether Ian Nairn's judgement on the former, 'a place for respect, not affection',[31] and Lionel Brett's assessment of public reaction to British architecture generally, which is extremely pertinent to Goldfinger's case, will remain valid: 'Unfortunately, precision is not a virtue the English admire. Character and atmosphere are the sort of words they use in praise, and the more indefinable a building's attributes, the more they like it. Of the two recognized ways of seeing, the classical tradition of formal discipline and the romantic vision of the building as sculpture, they keep veering back towards the romantic.'[32]

NOTES

1 *Architectural Design*, vol 33, January 1963, p8.
2 Ernö Goldfinger, *In Paris in the Twenties*, Pidgeon Audio Visual (London), [1980].
3 *The Architectural Review*, vol 115, May 1954, p341.
4 Quoted in Ernö Goldfinger, 'The Work of Auguste Perret', *Architectural Association Journal*, vol 70, January 1955, p150.
5 Description of Project for San Salvador in the *Ernö Goldfinger Papers*, Manuscripts & Archives Collection, British Architectural Library, RIBA. Unfortunately precise references cannot be given to the papers as at the time of writing they have yet to be fully sorted and numbered.
6 *Daily Sketch*, 31 December 1937.
7 Letter from Goldfinger to Frank Lloyd Wright, 13 December 1935, *Ernö Goldfinger Papers*, Manuscripts & Archives Collection, British Architectural Library, RIBA.
8 Gavin Stamp, 'Conversation with Ernö Goldfinger', *Thirties Society Journal*, no. 2, 1982, p23.
9 For an excellent analysis see Jeremy Gould, *Modern Houses in Britain, 1919-1939*, Society of Architectural Historians of Great Britain (Newcastle-upon-Tyne), 1977.
10 *House and Garden*, vol 10, October 1955, pp86-89.
11 Christopher Gotch, 'Nudging the National Trust', *Hampstead & Highgate Express & News*, 15 December 1972.
12 Henry-Russell Hitchcock, *Modern Architecture in England*, Museum of Modern Art (New York), 1937, p35.
13 *Architects' Journal*, vol 94, 23 October 1941, p271.
14 Lionel Esher, *A Broken Wave. The Rebuilding of England 1940-1980*, Allen Lane (London), 1981, p48.
15 *Builder*, vol 164, 19 March 1943, p271.
16 Both applications can be found in the *Ernö Goldfinger Papers*, Manuscripts & Archives Collection, British Architectural Library, RIBA.
17 Peter Rawsthorne, 'Seven Keys to Good Architecture', *Twentieth Century*, Winter 1963, pp147-48.
18 Ibid., p147.
19 *The Architectural Review*, vol 173, April 1983, p48.
20 Ibid.
21 Quoted in James Dunnett, 'Ernö Goldfinger: the Architect as Constructor', *The Architectural Review*, vol 173, April 1983, p46.
22 *Architects' Journal*, vol 126, 19 December 1957, p911.
23 Ibid.
24 *Architects' Journal*, vol 127, 16 January 1958, p99.
25 *New Statesman*, 10 May 1958.
26 See *Architectural Design*, vol 25, June 1955, pp187 and 192.
27 *Sunday Times*, 10 July 1960.
28 *Architects' Journal*, vol 161, 1 January 1975, p8.
29 'The Sensation of Space', *The Architectural Review*, vol 90, November 1941, pp129-31; 'Urbanism and Spatial Order', *The Architectural Review*, vol 90, December 1941, pp163-66; 'The Elements of Enclosed Space', *The Architectural Review*, vol 91, January 1942, pp5-8.
30 *RIBA Journal*, vol 95, February 1988, p90.
31 Ian Nairn, *Modern Buildings in London*, London Transport (London), 1964, p22.
32 *The Architectural Review*, vol 109, March 1951, p136.

FROM ABOVE, L TO R: Carr & Co, Birmingham (photo: de Burgh Galwey, 1956); 45-46 Albemarle Street, London (photo: Colin Westwood, 1958); Alexander Fleming House, London (photo: Sam Lambert, 1963); Trellick Tower, London (photo: Sam Lambert, 1973)

PLATES

1. Design for a lantern tower, 1924
2. Design for an architect's office, 1925
3. Design for law courts, 1925
4. Design for metal chair with sprung seat, 1925
5. Design for a railway terminus clock, 1926
6. Design for a shooting club, 1926
7. Design for a reservoir, 1926
8. Design for a commemorative chapel, 1926
9. Competition design for Palace of Justice, San Salvador, 1927
10. Design for an apartment block, Boulevard Raspail, Paris, 1927
11. Design for exterior of a salon for Helena Rubinstein, Grafton Street, London, 1926
12. Design for interior of a salon for Helena Rubinstein, London, 1926
13. Design for apartment interior, Rue de Babylone, Paris, 1929
14. Design for Bugatti showroom, Avenue des Champs-Elysées, Paris, 1929
15. Furniture designs, 1920s
16. Design for Skikda Palace Hotel, Philippeville, Algeria, 1929
17. Design for a flying club, 1932
18. Design for heliometer, 1933
19. Design for housing project for CIAM, 1933
20. Design for The Outlook, Le Touquet, 1934
21. Design for children's nesting chair, 1930s
22. Design for children's nursery display, Exhibition of Contemporary Industrial Design in the Home, Dorland Hall, London, 1934
23. Design for an expanding nursery school, 1934
24. Design for house at Broxted, Essex, 1937
25. Working drawing for shop, 2 Golders Green Road, London, 1936
26. Design for shop, 94 Wimpole Street, London, 1936
27. Design for Easiwork furniture, 1935
28. Design for display stand for Easiwork furniture, Ideal Home Exhibition, Olympia, London, 1937
29. Design for children's section in the British Pavilion for the 1937 Exposition Internationale des Arts et Techniques dans la Vie Moderne, Paris, 1936
30. Design for ICI stand, 1938 British Industries Fair, Olympia, London, 1937
31. Design for exterior, 1-3 Willow Road, Hampstead, London, c1938
32. Drawings for publication of 2 Willow Road, Hampstead, London, 1940
33. Design for interior of 3 Willow Road, Hampstead, London, 1938
34. Design for alterations to 13 West Hill, Highgate, London, 1939
35. Design for a standard nursery school, 1937
36. Drawing for publication of *Ideal Home* bungalow, 1941
37. Design for holiday and evacuation camp for families, 1940
38. Design for London 'Women's Parliament exhibition, Boots, Piccadilly Circus, London, 1943
39. Design for a radio in perspex for the Design Research Unit, 1945
40. Design for *The Cinema* exhibition, 1943
41. Engineers' drawing prepared by Ove N Arup for box-frame housing, c1944
42. Drawing showing a typical modern type of urban enclosure, 1942
43. Design for *Traffic* exhibition, 1944
44. Design for exhibition display for Friedman & Athill, 1945
45. Design for *Planning Your Kitchen* exhibition, 1944
46. Design for prefabricated housing project, 1945
47. Exhibition panel, *Planning Your Neighbourhood*, 1945
48. Design for the *Daily Worker*, 75 Farringdon Road, London, 1946
49. Drawing of prefabricated construction system for schools, 1950
50. Design for a kiosk for the Festival of Britain, South Bank, London, 1951
51. Design for a block of flats, 10 Regent's Park Road, London, 1954
52. Design for offices for Carr & Co, Cranmore Boulevard, Shirley, Birmingham, 1955
53. Design for 45-46 Albemarle Street, London, 1955
54. Contract drawing for 45-46 Albemarle Street, London, 1955
55. Design for office skyscraper, Moorgate, London, 1955
56. Design for housing, Hunton Bridge Road, Abbots Langley, 1956
57. Preliminary studies for *This Is Tomorrow* exhibition, Whitechapel Art Gallery, London, 1955-56
58. Design for a house in the Vale of Health, Hampstead, London, 1958
59. Design for office building, 69-70 Piccadilly, London, 1956
60. Design for Hille House, Watford, 1959
61. Design for Alexander Fleming House, Elephant and Castle, London, 1959
62. Design for Alexander Fleming House, Elephant and Castle, London, c1959
63. Preliminary studies for block D, Alexander Fleming House, London, 1962
64. Competition design for a shopping centre, Elephant and Castle, London, 1960
65. Working drawing for spiral staircase, Lime Tree House, Combe Hill Road, Malden, Surrey, 1961
66. Presentation drawing of office development, Bloomsbury Square, London, 1962
67. Preliminary designs for house, Bedford Street, Oxford, 1962
68. Design for Odeon, Elephant and Castle, London, 1965
69. Design for Odeon, Elephant and Castle, London, 1962
70. Working drawing for Odeon, Elephant and Castle, London, 1965
71. Preliminary study for flat layout, Rowlett Street housing, Poplar, London, 1962
72. Working drawing of sill details, Rowlett Street housing, London, 1966
73. Design for Rowlett Street housing, London, 1966
74. Design for the French Government Tourist Office and SNCF office, Piccadilly, London, 1961
75. Design for Teesdale, Westwood Road, Windlesham, Surrey, 1965
76. Design for Teesdale, Westwood Road, Windlesham, Surrey, 1977
77. Contract drawing for Edenham Street housing, North Kensington, London, 1967
78. Design for dwelling types, Edenham Street housing, London, 1976
79. Design for Edenham Street housing, London, 1967
80. Drawing of the French Government Tourist Office and SNCF office, 127 Avenue des Champs-Elysées, Paris, 1967

(All measurements in the following captions are given in millimetres)

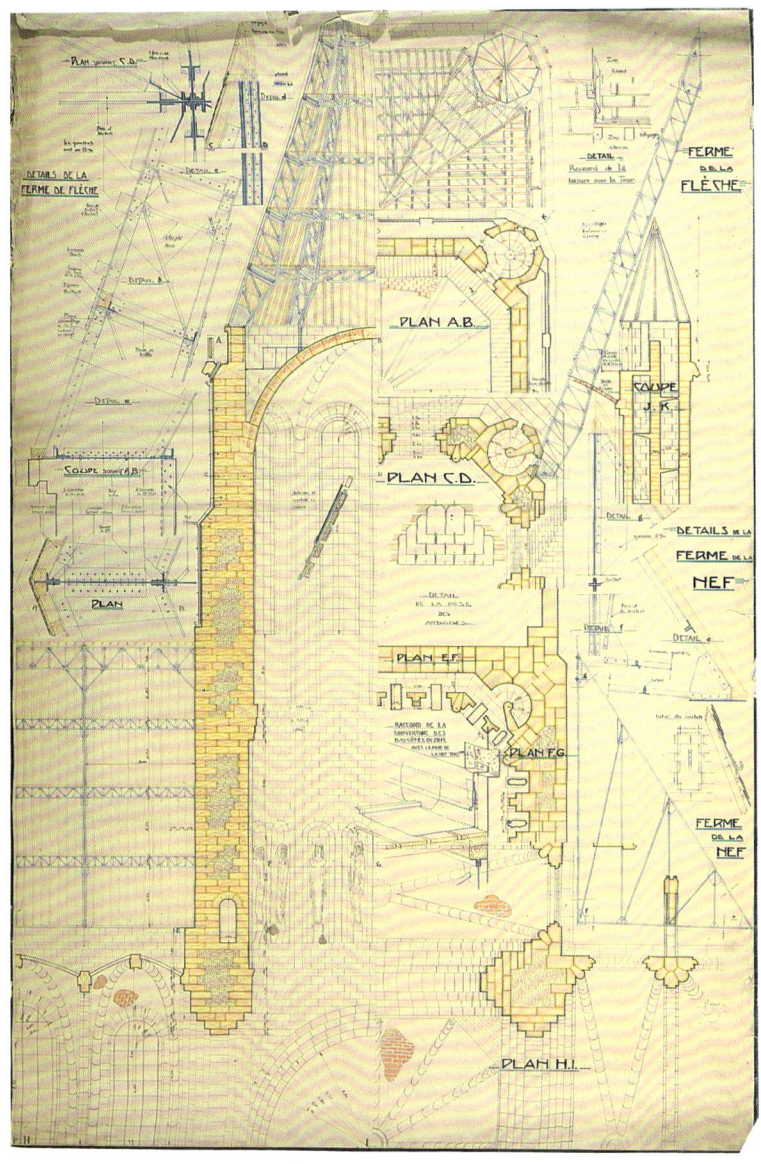

1. Design for a lantern tower, 1924

Pencil, pen, coloured pen and coloured washes (1045 × 700)

Goldfinger had been admitted to the Ecole des Beaux-Arts in June 1922 with the submission of a design, now lost, for an entrance to a catacomb in Greek Doric style. Although he was fiercely critical of the Ecole's conservatism it nevertheless provided him, as this early construction study vividly demonstrates, with a thorough grounding in construction and engineering techniques. The drawing was based on Goldfinger's study of a number of churches including San Andrea in Mantua and the cathedrals at Coutances, Ely and Lichfield, and of E Arnaud's *Cours d'architecture et de constructions civiles* (1922-23). Its style and manner of presentation show the clear influence of Viollet-le-Duc, a copy of whose *Dictionnaire raisonné de l'architecture française du XIe au XVIe siècle* (1854-68) Goldfinger possessed. An unswerving commitment to the principles of sound construction remained one of the hallmarks of Goldfinger's work throughout his long career.

2. Design for an architect's office, 1925

Pen and gouache (765 × 605)

This design, undertaken while in Perret's atelier and rejected by the Beaux-Arts jury, represents a surprising departure for Goldfinger, being an unlikely exercise in the Art Deco style made instantly fashionable by the Exposition Internationale des Arts Décoratifs et Industriels Modernes, Paris (1925), which Goldfinger had recently visited with his friend from the Café du Dôme, Adolf Loos. The opulent character of the interior, which could pass for a Hollywood film set of the 1930s, was in marked contrast to the austerity of Goldfinger's executed interiors of later in the decade. Similarly the free style of its drawing was later replaced by a more formally precise, geometrical idiom. Goldfinger soon dismissed Art Deco as a 'commercial thing', welcoming instead those very buildings at the exhibition, particularly Le Corbusier's Pavillon de l'Esprit Nouveau, Konstantin Melnikov's Soviet Pavilion and its Japanese counterpart, which marked a radical departure from the glitteringly lavish Deco confections which dominated the site.

3. Design for law courts, 1925

Pen and wash with red gouache (255 × 1035)

In 1925 Goldfinger was instrumental, together with a number of other students, in forming the Atelier Perret. The Ecole des Beaux-Arts was composed of a number of such independent ateliers run by the students who were free to choose their own *chef d'atelier*. Under his guidance projects were sent anonymously to the Grand Jury either to gain credits (*mention*) or to be rejected (*four*). It was usual for the *chef d'atelier* also to be a member of the jury but Perret's involvement in his brothers' contracting business and his failure to complete the Beaux-Arts course and become *Architecte DPLG* saw him ostracised by the architectural establishment. Although under Tony Garnier's influence the jury during this period gradually came to accept designs such as this in reinforced concrete, its strong preference remained for monumental classical projects in stone and this design, heavily influenced by Perret, was rejected.

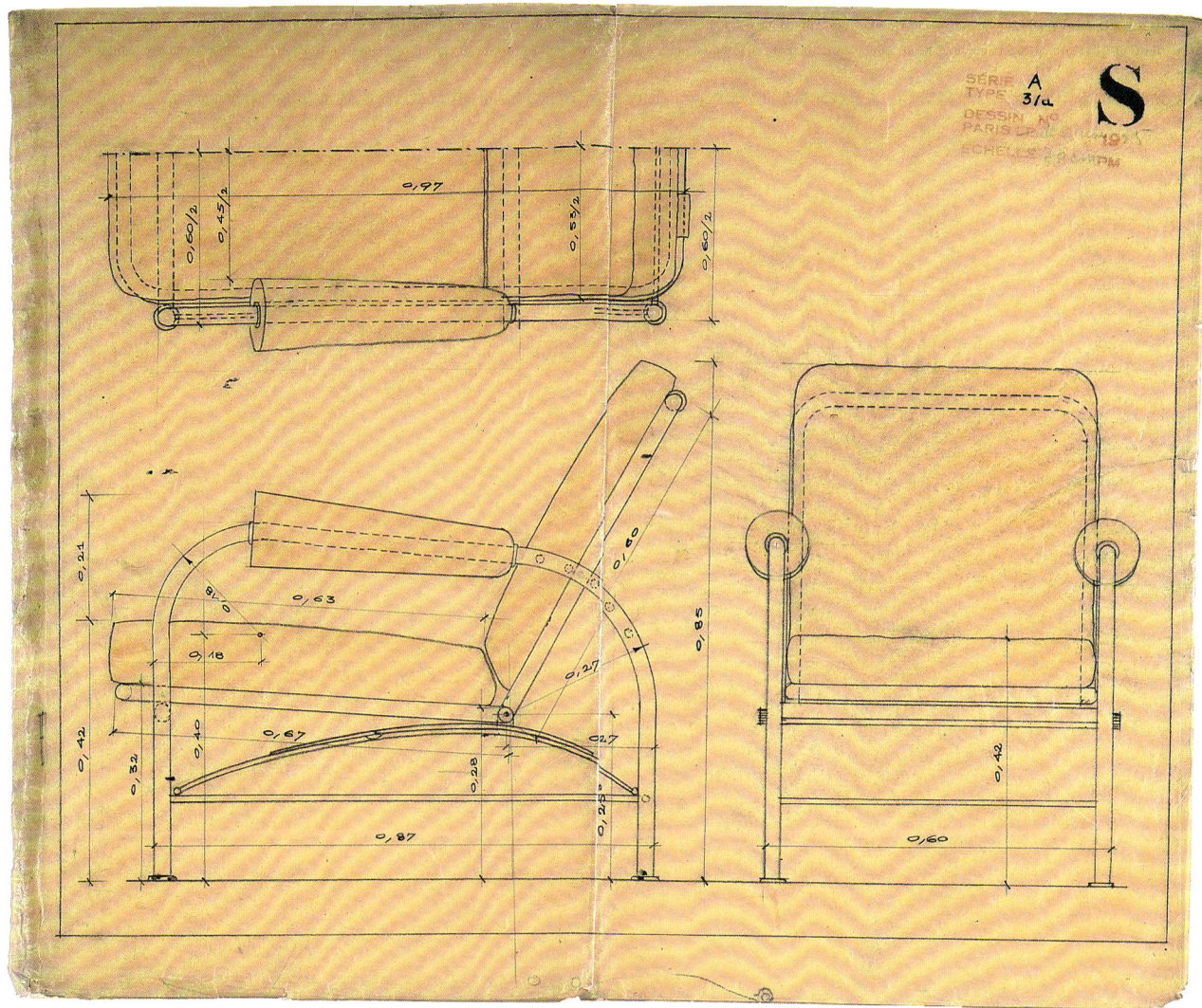

4. Design for metal chair with sprung seat, 1925

Pen and yellow crayon on tracing paper (320 × 400)

This armchair in leather and chrome steel, designed with his partner András Szivessy, was constructed, Goldfinger said, so that you could throw yourself into it. The back could be adjusted to a horizontal position and the junctions were bolted together to allow easy disassembly of the frame. In common with other Goldfinger furniture designs of the period this is characterised by a willingness to experiment with new materials and reflected his strong belief that furniture should be ergonomically designed rather than 'go with the room'. It was one of a number of the partnership's executed schemes featured in Roger Ginsburger's *Junge französische Architektur* published in 1930. Furniture design continued to be an important part of Goldfinger's work, and in 1951 he edited a book on the subject, *British Furniture Today*.

5. Design for a railway terminus clock, 1926

Pencil, pen, red and blue gouache, Chinese white and sepia air brush (740 × 1060)

Frustrated by the continued rejection of his designs Goldfinger left Perret's atelier in 1926 and joined that of Alphonse Alexandre Defrasse, noted for his knowledge of classical architecture and a pillar of the Beaux-Arts establishment. This successful 'projet Godeboeuf' is marked by its use of vivid colour – an often overlooked facet of Goldfinger's work – which together with the decorative elements around the borders imparts a strongly Constructivist feel to the drawing. Goldfinger always vigorously rebutted suggestions that his work was influenced by Russian Constructivism but he was impressed by Melnikov's Soviet Pavilion in 1925, the roofscape of which may have influenced his first unexecuted scheme for Humphrey Waterfield's house at Broxted (1936), and he also had access to copies of *L'Architecture vivante* which regularly published articles on the movement.

6. Design for a shooting club, 1926

Pencil, pen, red and blue gouache, Chinese white and sepia wash (625 × 1100)

Recalling his time in Perret's atelier Goldfinger wrote: 'We bravely sent in our projects every two months. The new Patron came twice a week, on Tuesdays and Fridays, in the afternoon, to look at our projects, to criticise, to talk to us about the Parthenon and about the mosques at Constantinople, about Chartres and Amiens and the Sainte-Chapelle – he had just built the church at Le Raincy himself – about shuttering for reinforced concrete . . .' This design, unusually accepted by the Beaux-Arts jury, shows Goldfinger's increasingly assured handling of Perret's method of using the exposed reinforced concrete skeleton as the determinant element in the composition. The prominent spiral staircase, which was to become a recurrent motif in Goldfinger's work providing a sensuous contrast to its essentially rectilinear nature, echoes that of Perret's 1924 Tour d'Orientation at Grenoble.

7. Design for a reservoir, 1926

Pen and sepia air brush (560 × 980)

This was the last project Goldfinger submitted to the Beaux-Arts jury whilst in the Atelier Perret and as with so many others it was rejected. In addition to the spiral staircase, the design contains several other elements that were to reappear in Goldfinger's later work. The rectangular water tower above the main reservoir, for example, foreshadows that at Carr & Co, whilst the row of small square windows puncturing the facade (derived perhaps from the reconstruction of Pergamum published in 1900 by Emmanuel Pontremoli, another Beaux-Arts *chef d'atelier*) is a device which is repeated in Goldfinger's design for a flying club, in The Outlook at Le Touquet, in an enlarged version at Willow Road, and finally in the Odeon at the Elephant and Castle.

8. Design for a commemorative chapel, 1926

Pencil, pen, grey wash with Chinese white, gold paint and gouache (990 × 535)

This drawing was submitted for the Prix de la Fondation Rougevin, a competition 'd'ornement et d'ajustement'. The conditions called for the design of a chapel consecrated to the memory of an illustrious cardinal which was to contain a tomb executed in white marble and a sculpture of the prelate represented in a suitably dignified manner. Goldfinger's circular design, which was rejected, is reminiscent of an earlier similarly dramatic but accepted project for a thermal spring (1925) and draws its inspiration from the visionary schemes of French eighteenth-century architects such as Etienne-Louis Boullée and Claude-Nicolas Ledoux.

9. Competition design for Palace of Justice, San Salvador, 1927

Pen and pencil on tracing paper (540 × 960)

In 1927 with Szivessy Goldfinger was commissioned by a firm of contractors to prepare drawings for an international competition to design a university science faculty and law courts in San Salvador. The designs for the latter, which bear certain similarities to Perret's competition entry for the League of Nations building at Geneva (1926-27), are among the most impressive of Goldfinger's early schemes. They also reveal what was to become a characteristic concern of Goldfinger for the insolation of buildings. A key element of the design was thus to protect the building's occupants from direct sunlight and while the offices opened onto internal patios, the courtrooms and large central hall were lit indirectly by brises-soleil. The palace's reinforced concrete frame was carefully calculated to be earthquake resistant and in the description submitted to the assessors Goldfinger argued: 'This economic and rational mode of construction is absolutely not contrary to great monumental architecture. There are numerous recent constructions for the French state like this. The rigidity of the colonnade is a dignified expression of the grandiose austerity of a Palace of Justice.' The assessors were not persuaded and the competition was won by the Belgian architect, Camille Damman.

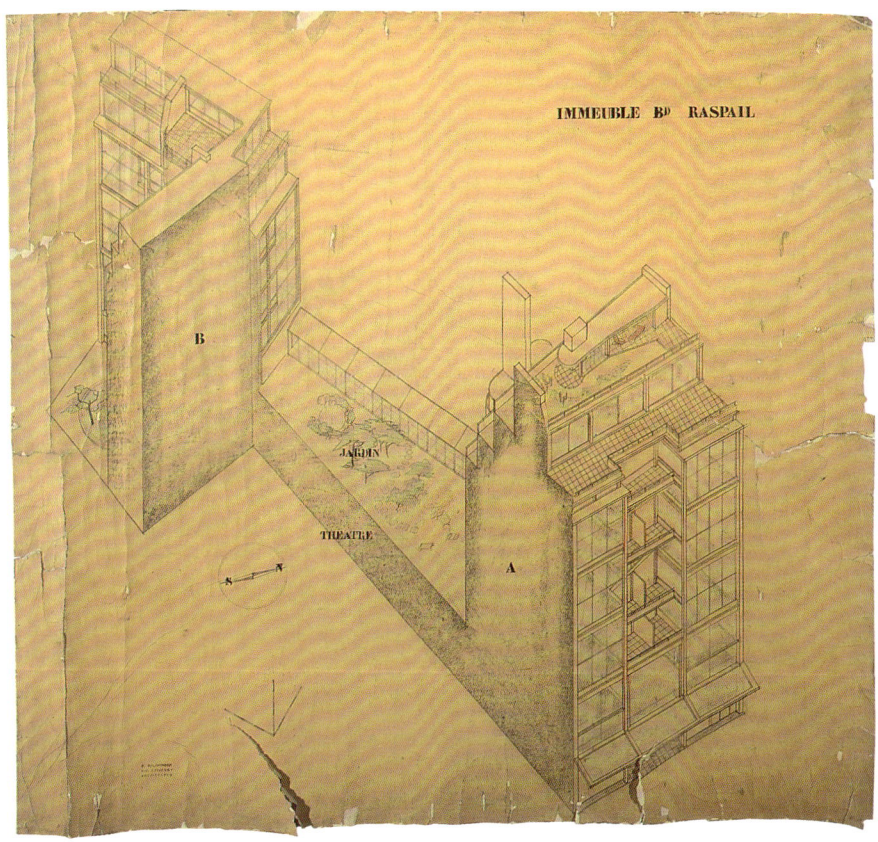

10. Design for an apartment block, Boulevard Raspail, Paris, for M and Mme Edward Titus, 1927

Pencil, pen, charcoal and coloured crayon on backed tracing paper (735 × 790)

This was one of a number of projects undertaken at this time by Goldfinger and Szivessy for the celebrated beautician, Helena Rubinstein, and her bookseller husband, Edward Titus. These included another apartment block in the Rue de l'Ambre, a bookshop, glass furniture for Helena Rubinstein's salons, and her London showroom. This block was never built, but the partnership remained reliant on its ability to attract a steady stream of such rich and prestigious clients.

11. Design for exterior of a salon for Helena Rubinstein, Grafton Street, London, 1926

Pencil, pen, charcoal and pastel on backed tracing paper (950 × 655)

Hailed by the architect and critic, Sir Charles Reilly, as 'the best of the examples of small single shops of a modern kind I have been able to collect', the Helena Rubinstein salon, with its simple, unadorned facade and elegant lines stood in stark contrast to the predominantly neo-Georgian shop designs of the period which Goldfinger later described as all being 'painted green. Everything was fake Queen Anne, like Fortnum & Mason's.' The commission, which Goldfinger obtained via an American girlfriend who worked

for Rubinstein, proved difficult. The client was unhappy with the designs, not least with the repeated illuminated lettering shown in this perspective which she regarded as in bad taste and in execution it was therefore simplified to a discreet band along the fascia. In the end Goldfinger was forced to sue his client for his fee using as his lawyer a neighbour and future client, Suzanne Blum, a student at the time but later famous as the confidante of the Duchess of Windsor.

12. Design for interior of a salon for Helena Rubinstein, Grafton Street, London, 1926

Charcoal and pastel on tracing paper (935 × 575)

The streamlined nature of the interior caused complaints from the client who wrote that though attractive it had 'just a slight appearance of an operating theatre', while the bemused draughtsmen of Frederick Sage & Co, the shop-fitters, sought to add decorative elements to the drawings in the mistaken belief that Goldfinger had omitted to do so. The architect politely explained to his client (in a letter written before he had mastered English): 'We don't believe in a decoration applicated arbitrary. That is to say there is no possibility to hang on a few columns, or false panneling, a few curtins, to hide . . . corners, to do all the plastering & all this innumerous procedings of so-called classical architecture. The stuff we are doing is simple and plain and gets all its value of the balance of its proportions of the perfect satisfaction it gives in fonction, of the materials . . . in their right place.' The shop, finally built in conjunction with the London architect, Ashley Benjamin, no longer exists.

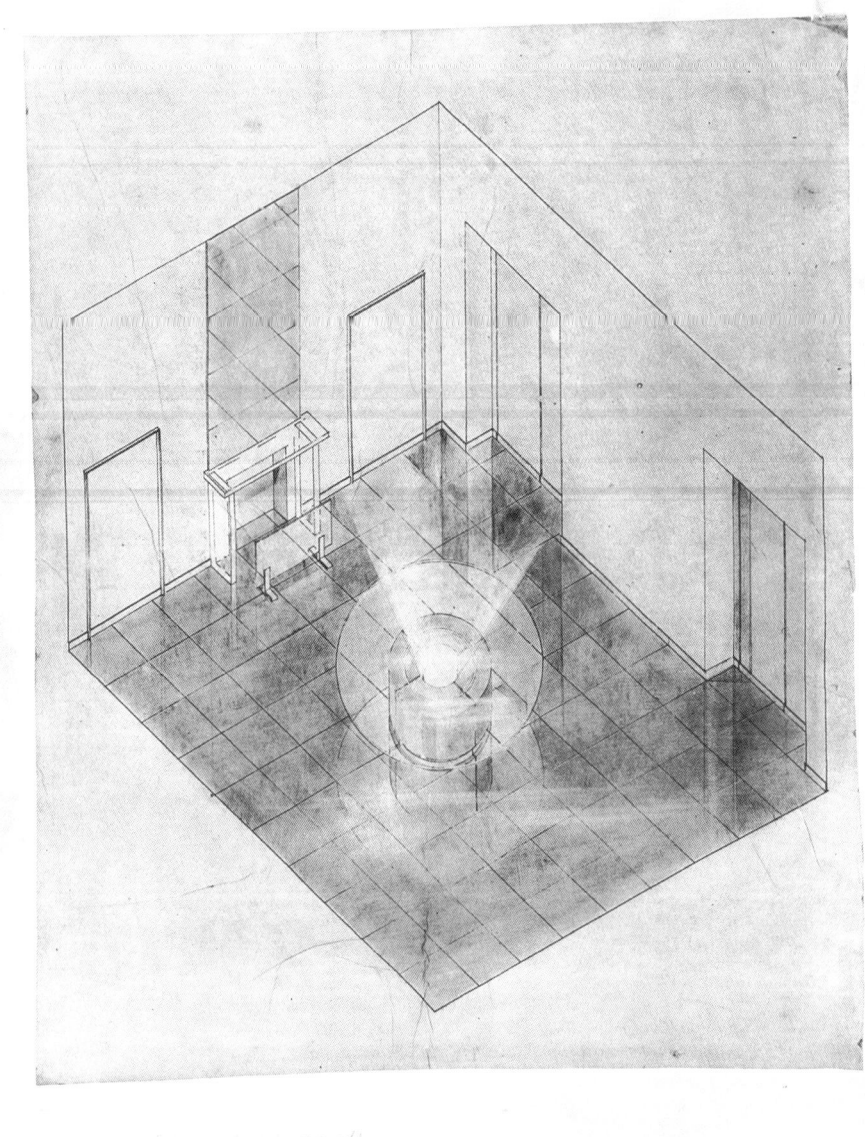

13. Design for apartment interior, Rue de Babylone, Paris, for Robert de Veyrac, 1929
Pen and pencil on backed tracing paper (730 × 555)

This apartment interior, boasting a glass table illuminated from below and an equally improbable glass fireplace, was commissioned by the interior designer, Robert de Veyrac, but was later occupied by Madame Cuttoli, one of Goldfinger's main clients at the time.

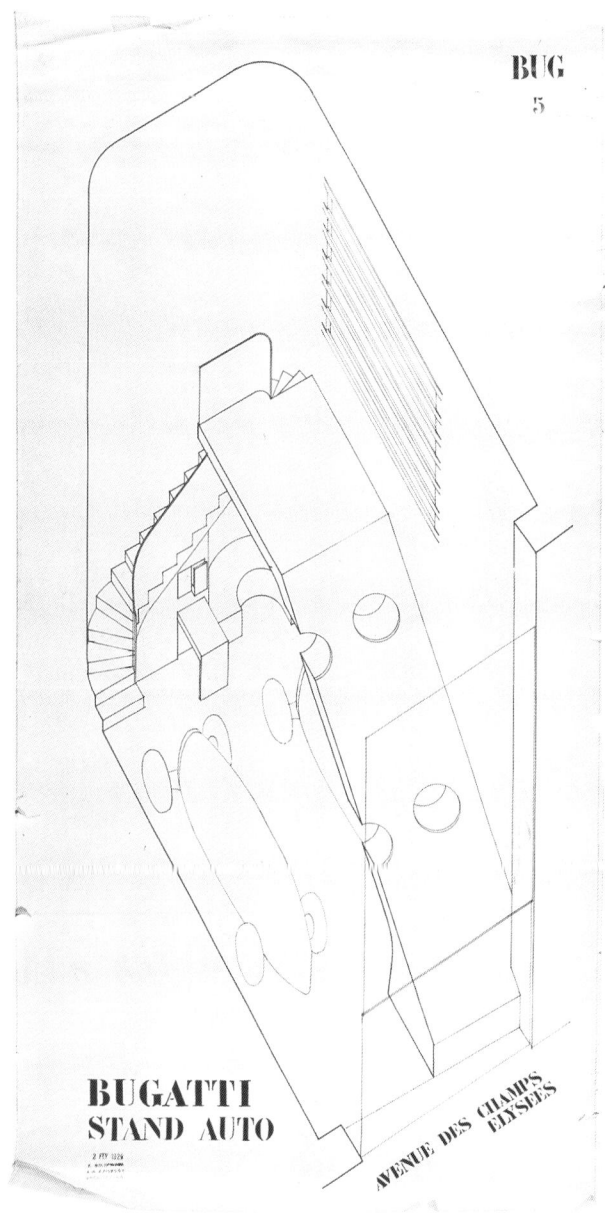

14. Design for Bugatti showroom, Avenue des Champs-Elysées, Paris, 1929

Pen on tracing paper (900 × 450)

Like other Modernist architects Goldfinger was obsessed with cars, owning several fine examples, and including numerous depictions of them in his drawings, as well as making designs for car chassis. This drawing illustrates Goldfinger's increasing use of the axonometric, a pictorial convention favoured by adherents of the Modern Movement, which had first been used in France in the eighteenth century and subsequently popularised by one of the formative influences on Goldfinger, Auguste Choisy, in his *Histoire de l'architecture* (1899).

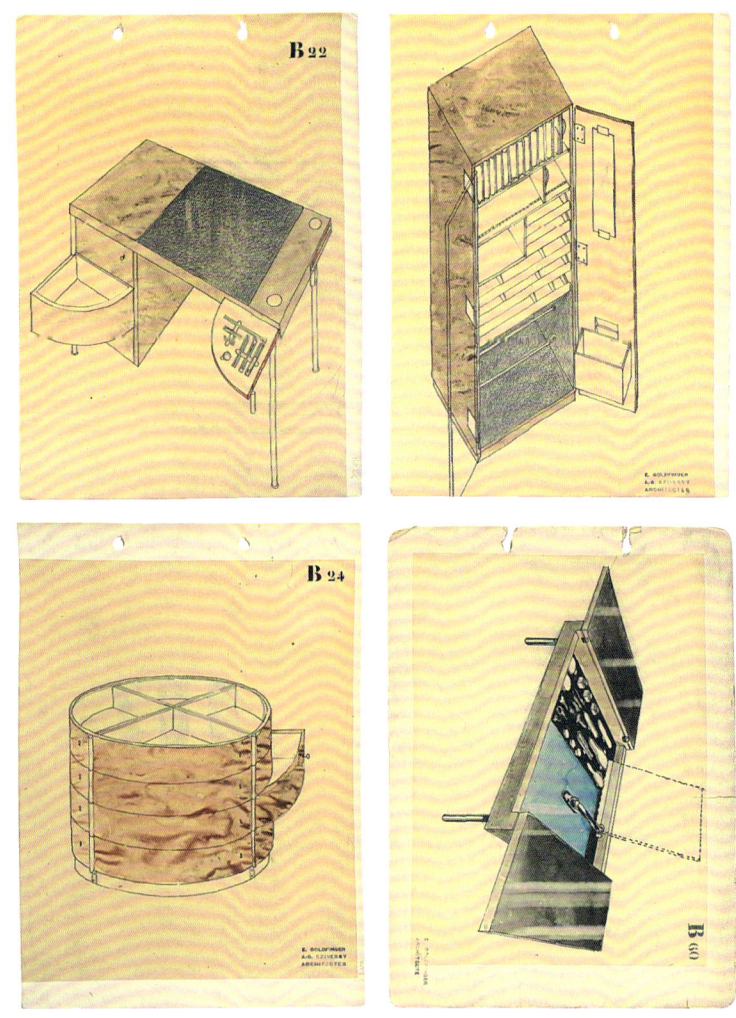

15. Furniture designs, 1920s

Pen and coloured washes (300 × 220 each)

Goldfinger and Szivessy drew up many designs for furniture in the 1920s, some of which were incorporated into their apartment interiors. Of particular interest was their 1927 competition design for the Austrian manufacturers, Thonet, for a clothes cupboard with space at the top to 'file away' laundered shirts and a ventilated dirty laundry bin at the bottom.

16. Design for Skikda Palace Hotel, Philippeville, Algeria, for Senator Cuttoli, 1929

Pencil, coloured washes, Chinese white and sepia air brush (600 × 1000)

In 1929 Goldfinger was invited to Algeria for three months by the mayor of Philippeville, Senator Cuttoli, and asked to draw up plans for the development and extension of the town in conjunction with the architect and urban planner, Louis-Georges Pineau. These included low-cost flats and houses as well as this reinforced concrete hotel overlooking the sea, a second project for which followed in 1930. Although in the end nothing was built, the scheme was important in helping Goldfinger to refine his ideas on urban planning.

17. Design for a flying club, 1932

Pencil and charcoal on backed tracing paper (630 × 1300)

In 1932 Goldfinger finally acquired his *DPLG* with this project for a flying club in reinforced concrete with plain Burgundian brick infilling. The design grew out of an earlier abortive competition scheme for the town planning of Angers developed with Georges Meyer from 1930 onwards and was submitted to the Beaux-Arts jury while Goldfinger was in the atelier of the architectural historian, Georges Gromort.

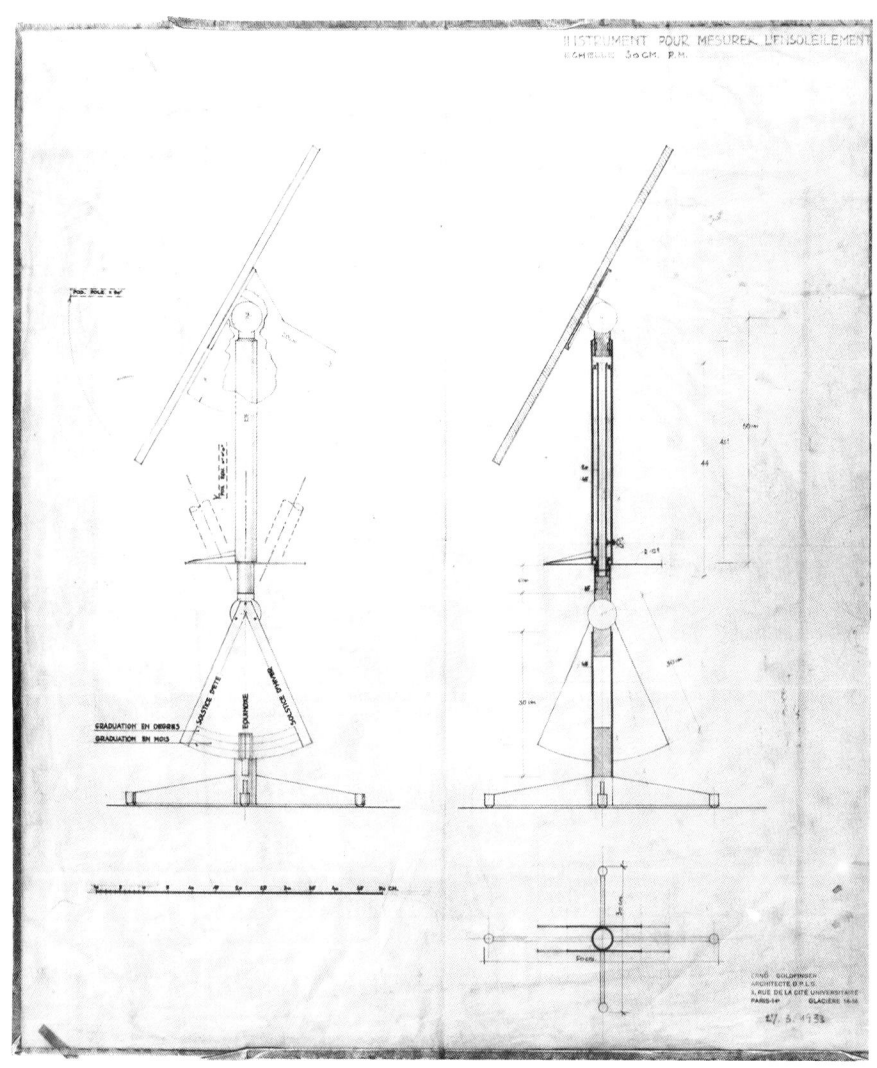

18. Design for heliometer, 1933

Pencil and pen on tracing paper (645 × 550)

Goldfinger attached particular importance to the insolation of buildings, to their penetration by sunlight and the shadows they cast on their surroundings. In order to be able to test these effects scientifically, he constructed, with the advice of the Paris Observatory, his heliometer, a 4-feet 6-inches high instrument on which a model 2 feet 6 inches by 2 feet 6 inches could be inclined and rotated to simulate the earth's movements in relation to the sun's rays. These latter were in turn simulated by a parabolic reflector 1 foot in diameter and fitted with a 300-watt lamp which was placed 12 to 15 feet away from the heliometer on to which it was shone. The model could also be positioned on the heliometer so as to simulate any latitude from the poles to the equator. Looking at the drawing the upper segment is for setting the latitude, the middle disc the hours, and the lower segment the seasons. One of the first projects to be tested using this device was the CIAM housing scheme. Goldfinger's concern for the effects of sunlight, motivated in part by the Modern Movement's reaction to the gloominess of many existing buildings and the equation of sunshine with good health, continued with his development and use of the photobolic screen.

19. Design for housing project for CIAM, 1933

Print with pencil, red pen, green and grey washes and sepia air brush added (675 × 420)

In 1933 Goldfinger participated as its French secretary in the Congrès International d'Architecture Moderne (CIAM) mainly held on board the liner, Patris II, sailing between Marseilles and Athens. The Congrès has achieved fame largely because of Le Corbusier's seminal *Athens Charter* although this was not in fact published until ten years later and then only anonymously. The conference included an exhibition of architectural projects and Goldfinger's was a self-contained 23-storey housing block with facilities such as nursery and infants' schools and a communal restaurant – a prototype perhaps of Le Corbusier's famous Unité d'Habitation at Marseilles (1952). An interesting feature of Goldfinger's design was its division on the day and night principle with two hundred people, mostly women and children, expected to occupy the building during the day and seven hundred at night. Later Goldfinger buildings such as the *Ideal Home* bungalow of 1941 also incorporated this principle.

20. Design for The Outlook, Le Touquet, for M Lahousse, 1934

Print with pencil and coloured washes added (310 × 380)

Goldfinger designed a new free-standing studio, his first complete building, as well as remodelling the adjacent country house, for his client, M Lahousse. The conversion included the refurbishment of the living room shown here with furniture of his own design. In the foreground are Goldfinger's Safari chair and accompanying stool, originally designed in 1929 and subsequently developed for the American fashion model and photographer, Lee Miller. The chair in leather and wood and based on the traditional North African desert chair was to prove one of Goldfinger's most successful and enduring designs undergoing numerous modifications over the years.

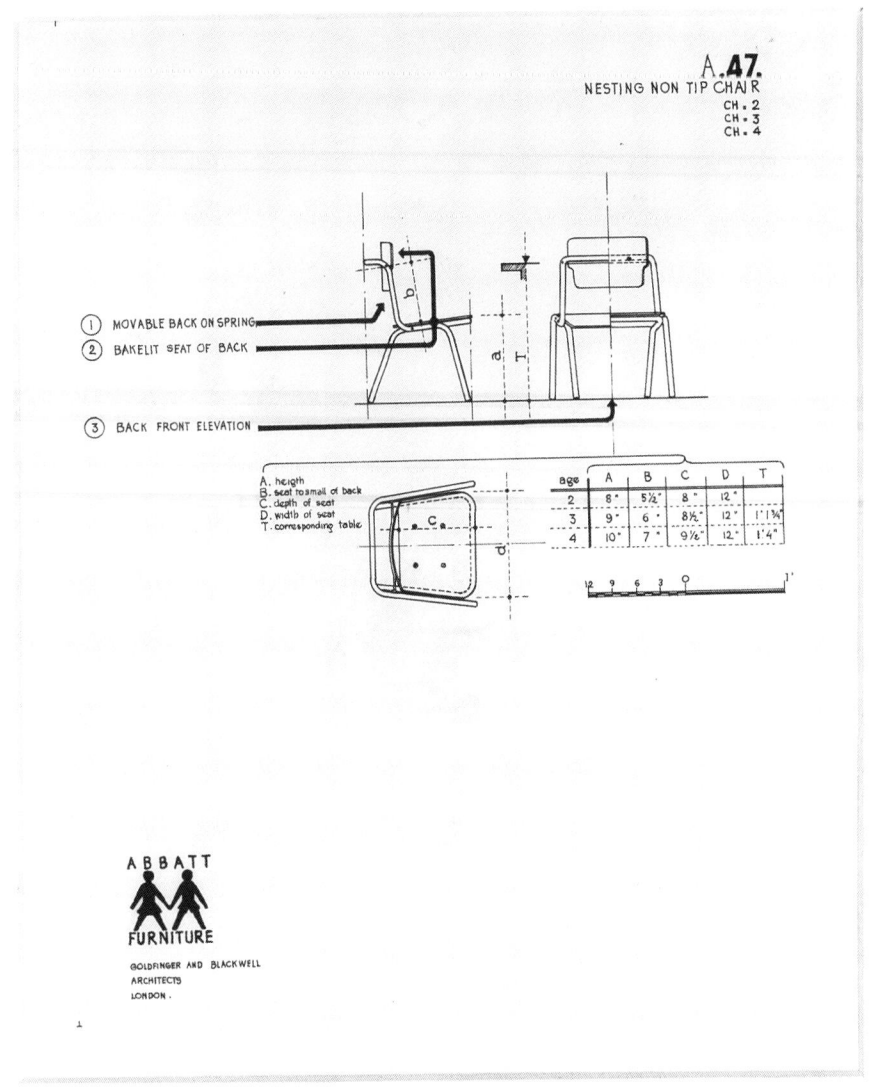

21. Design for children's nesting chair for Abbatt Furniture, 1930s

Pen on tracing paper (320 × 270)

With two small children of his own in the 1930s, Goldfinger realised that many things children could and should do for themselves in the home were prevented by the presence of furniture and fittings solely designed for adults. Accordingly he scaled down several of his own furniture designs for use by children, including, as shown here, his Entas stacking chair, writing: 'I'm not arguing for a toy world in the home, or anywhere else. We don't want to set the child apart. But we do want a home and school world he can inhabit and handle. One which will lead to the world he'll have to inhabit and deal with later.'

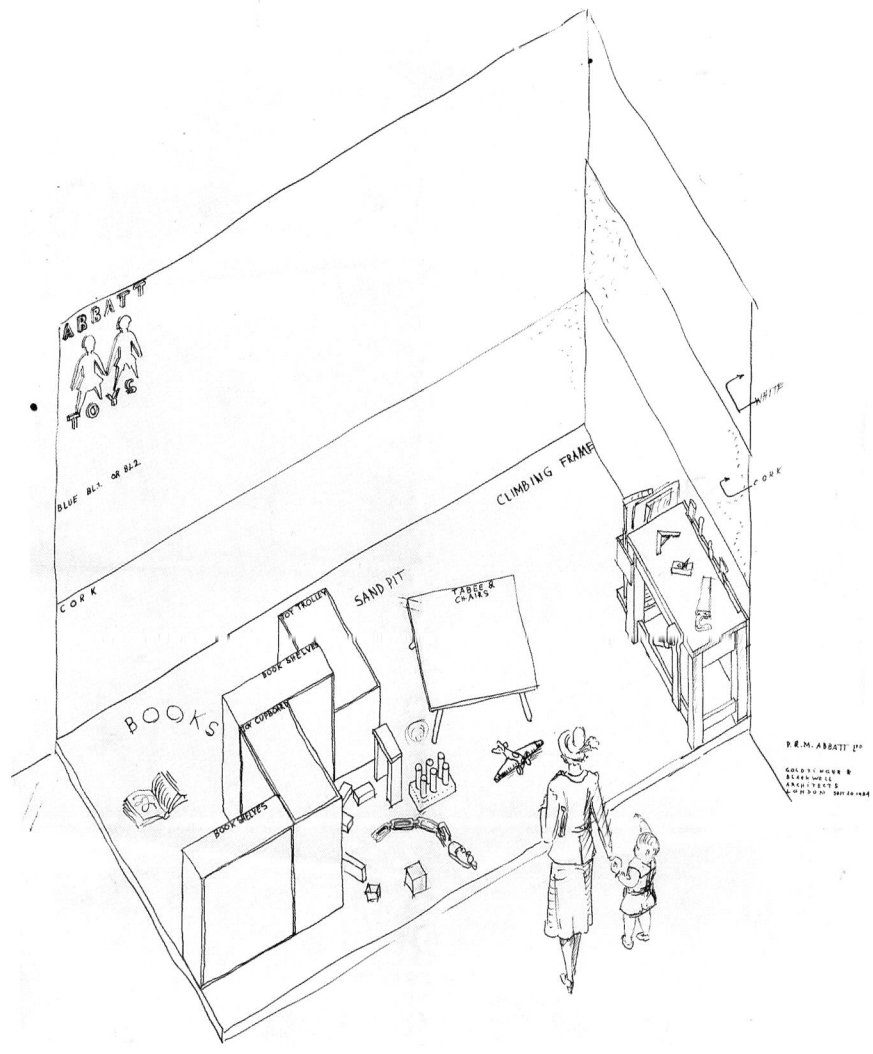

22. Design for children's nursery display, Exhibition of Contemporary Industrial Design in the Home, Dorland Hall, London, for P & M Abbatt Ltd, 1934

Pen on tracing paper (595 × 495)

Goldfinger had begun designing toys for Paul and Marjorie Abbatt whilst still in Paris and on his arrival in England he and his wife, Ursula, were engaged to design this exhibit for the Exhibition of Contemporary Industrial Design in the Home, the second such show to be held at Dorland Hall under the guiding hand of Oliver Hill. The exhibit, which included some of the toys designed by Goldfinger, well illustrated the pioneering work of the Abbatts in introducing the notion of creative play. Drawing on ideas advocated by Montessori and Fröbel and heavily influenced by HG Wells's seminal *Floor Games*

(1913), the Abbatts believed that play should not merely be about amusement but that properly designed toys which stimulated the child's imagination were essential to its psychological and physical development. From their premises in Tavistock Square, shared with the Nursery Schools Association, they sold a range of brightly coloured toys, specialising particularly in large wooden bricks. To the right of the exhibit can be seen their carpenter's bench on which children aged four could hammer and file pieces of wood and those of six and upwards could use specially designed small tools such as saws.

23. Design for an expanding nursery school for the Nursery Schools Association, 1934

Pencil and coloured crayon on tracing paper (315 × 505)

During the 1930s a vigorous campaign was mounted to secure proper nursery education for children aged from two to five. As there was no statutory requirement for local authorities to provide such education most was carried out, often in unsuitable accommodation, by private bodies like the Nursery Schools Association. The scale of the problem was daunting – in 1938 it was calculated that five thousand new nursery schools of one hundred children each would be required – and although interesting schools in a Modernist idiom were built by Max Fry, Elizabeth Denby and their team at Kensal House (1936), and Samuel & Harding at Dulwich (1937), these were one-offs that did little to overcome the major obstacle to adequate provision, cost. In an attempt to tackle the problem the Nursery Schools Association commissioned Goldfinger to design a cheap, standardised school which, unlike most existing educational buildings, which were solidly built and 'permanent', would be light, flexible and capable of being easily extended. In line with progressive educational theory and the contemporary belief in the beneficial effects of fresh air, its classroom could be opened up on one side. The scheme, though unbuilt, was one of the first to suggest that prefabrication could provide the key to reduced costs.

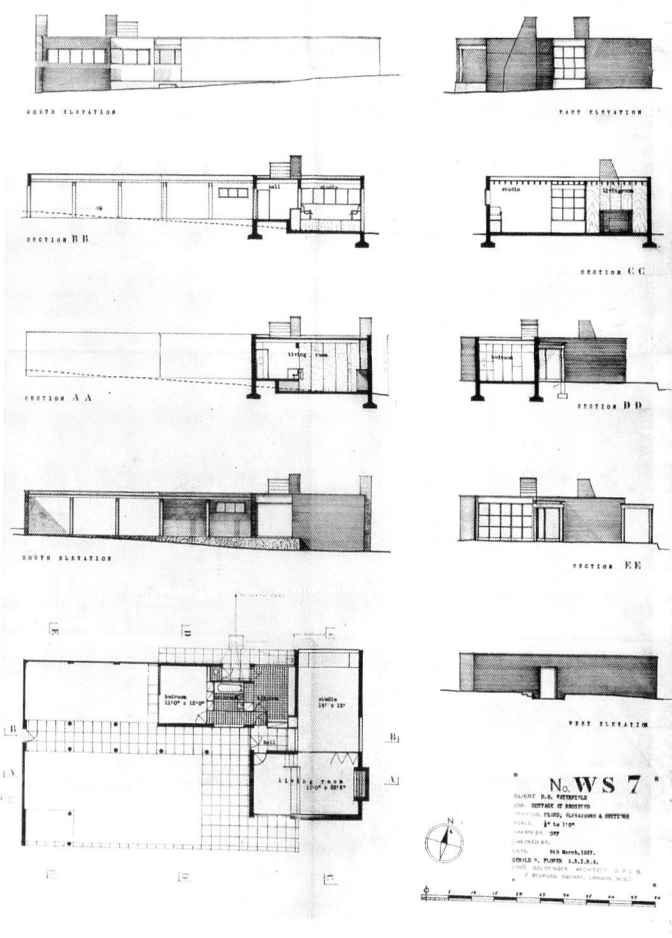

24. Design for house at Broxted, Essex, for DH Waterfield, 1937

Drawn by Gerald W Flower. Pen and pencil on tracing paper (670 × 460)

Executed in conjunction with Gerald Flower, this house for the artist, Humphrey Waterfield, was built of red brick with an outside covered way formed by timber posts and beams and covered with corrugated asbestos cement sheeting. The treatment of the roof caused the architects considerable trouble, an earlier design with a double monopitch having been abandoned, and the flat roof of the new design being opposed by neighbours. Waterfield wrote to Flower: 'Alas and alack for all your Modernismus! The agreement came today and to my horror there was a clause that . . . the outside must conform to the "old Essex type" of exterior! . . . It appears that he [the site vendor] will see the studio from his new house and must have tiles or thatch. His own affair he showed me the drawings for & it looked a masterpiece of stockbrokers gothic . . .' The house, which was featured in the second edition of FRS Yorke's *The Modern House* (1944), was later altered by Flower.

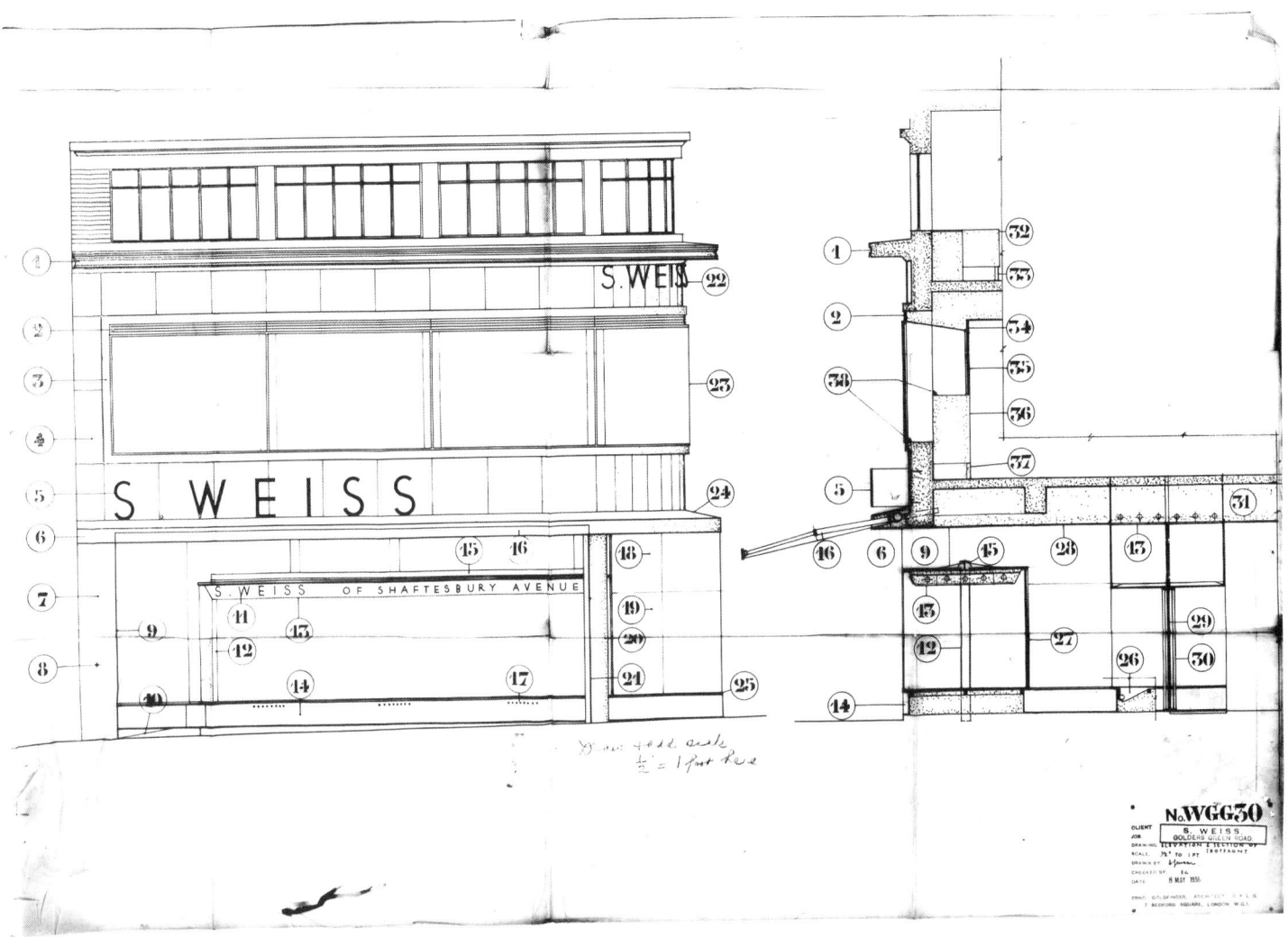

25. Working drawing for shop, 2 Golders Green Road, London, for S Weiss Ltd, 1936

Drawn by Rolf Jensen. Pen on tracing paper (610 × 890)

This shop originated in designs drawn up by Goldfinger in 1935 for a hairdressing salon on the site which had first been acquired by PH Edwards, a local property developer with whom Goldfinger was also involved in a scheme to build a hotel and houses in the Cuckmere Valley in Sussex. The site was finally taken over by the lingerie firm of S Weiss for whom Goldfinger designed another shop in Shaftesbury Avenue in 1951. The Golders Green branch, the curved frontage of which recalled Eric Mendelsohn's Petersdorff store,

Breslau (1927), contained a number of characteristic Goldfinger touches. Chief among these were its recessed frontage and the use within for indirect illumination of silvered glass asymmetrical uplighters which Goldfinger had employed on earlier projects such as the studio he designed for Richard Wyndham in Paris in 1930. *The Architectural Review* observed: 'The whole effect has a slightly fashionable well-groomed air, most appropriate to the subject.' The building survives although much altered.

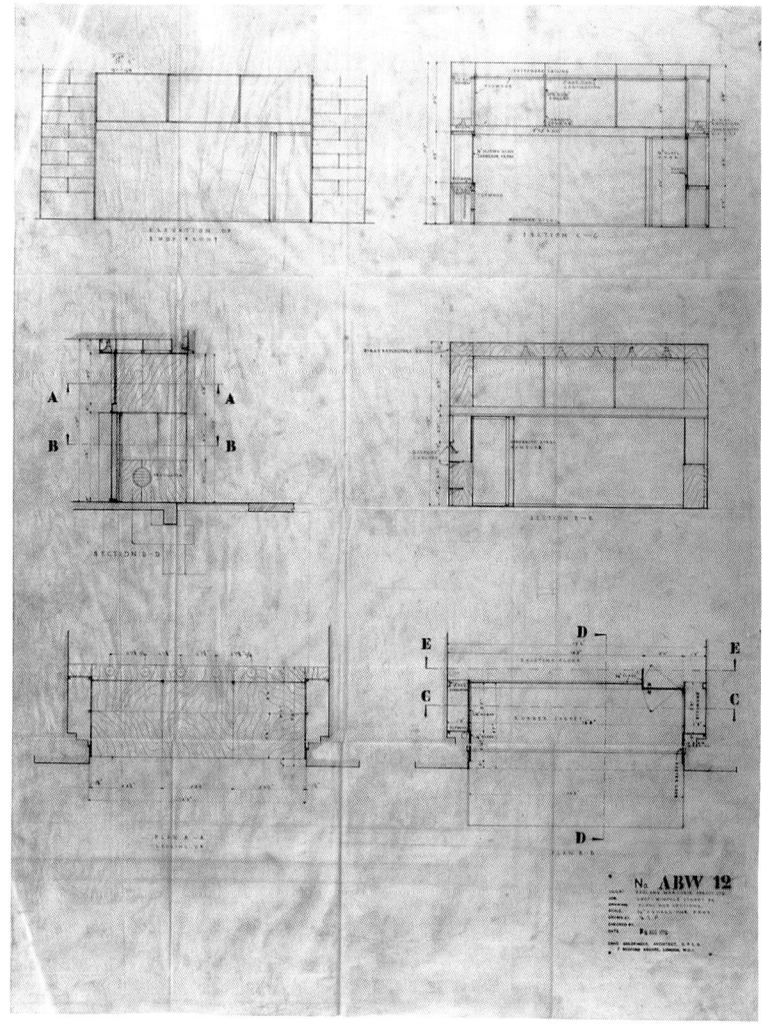

26. Design for shop, 94 Wimpole Street, London, for P & M Abbatt Ltd, 1936

Drawn by Donald E Pilcher. Pencil and pen on tracing paper (935 × 710)

The new shop which Goldfinger designed for Paul and Marjorie Abbatt, whose previous premises had been in Tavistock Square, was one of his most impressive pre-war works. Unfortunately only a handful of original drawings survive in the RIBA collection and the shop has been demolished. As it was located in a narrow, busy street, its main window was recessed by 7 feet thus forming a protective lobby for customers. This was flanked on either side by mahogany ply display cases and cork notice boards attached to the side pillars. The large unbroken expanse of glass with its stylish grey cellulosed steel surround, the graceful lettering in blue and white, and the frameless plate glass entrance door etched with the Abbatt's striking logo (also designed by Goldfinger) were effortlessly combined to impart an air of refined elegance to the exterior.

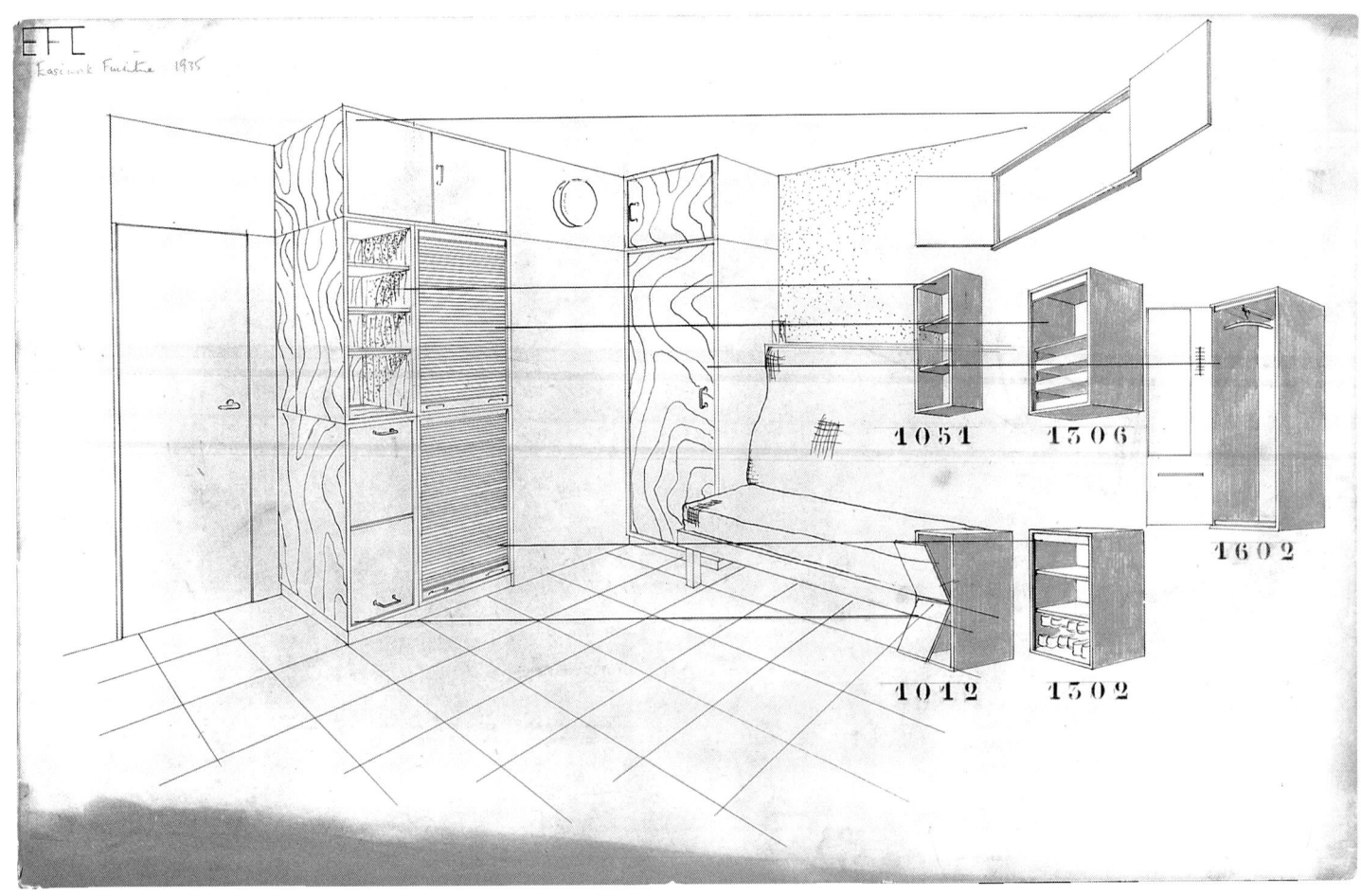

27. Design for Easiwork furniture, 1935

Pen and pencil on board (315 × 505)

The furniture manufacturers, Easiwork, had been established by a Canadian publisher, CEW Grove, who, having emigrated to Britain after the First World War, tried to set up a firm selling vacuum cleaners but was put out of business by Hoover. Instead he turned to selling kitchen cabinets and then to other furniture, commissioning designs for standard elements from architects including Raymond McGrath and Goldfinger. This collaboration resulted in EFE – the Easiwork Furniture Elements – based on a standard module of 3 feet by 2 feet by 17 inches which reduced manufacturing costs and allowed 'ample space for the progressive designer to achieve individuality of the arrangement of these units'. Goldfinger's designs, though giving the appearance of simplicity, were well thought through and an outcome of his long-standing interest in well organised and rational storage which had begun with contributions to *L'Organisation ménagère* in the late 1920s.

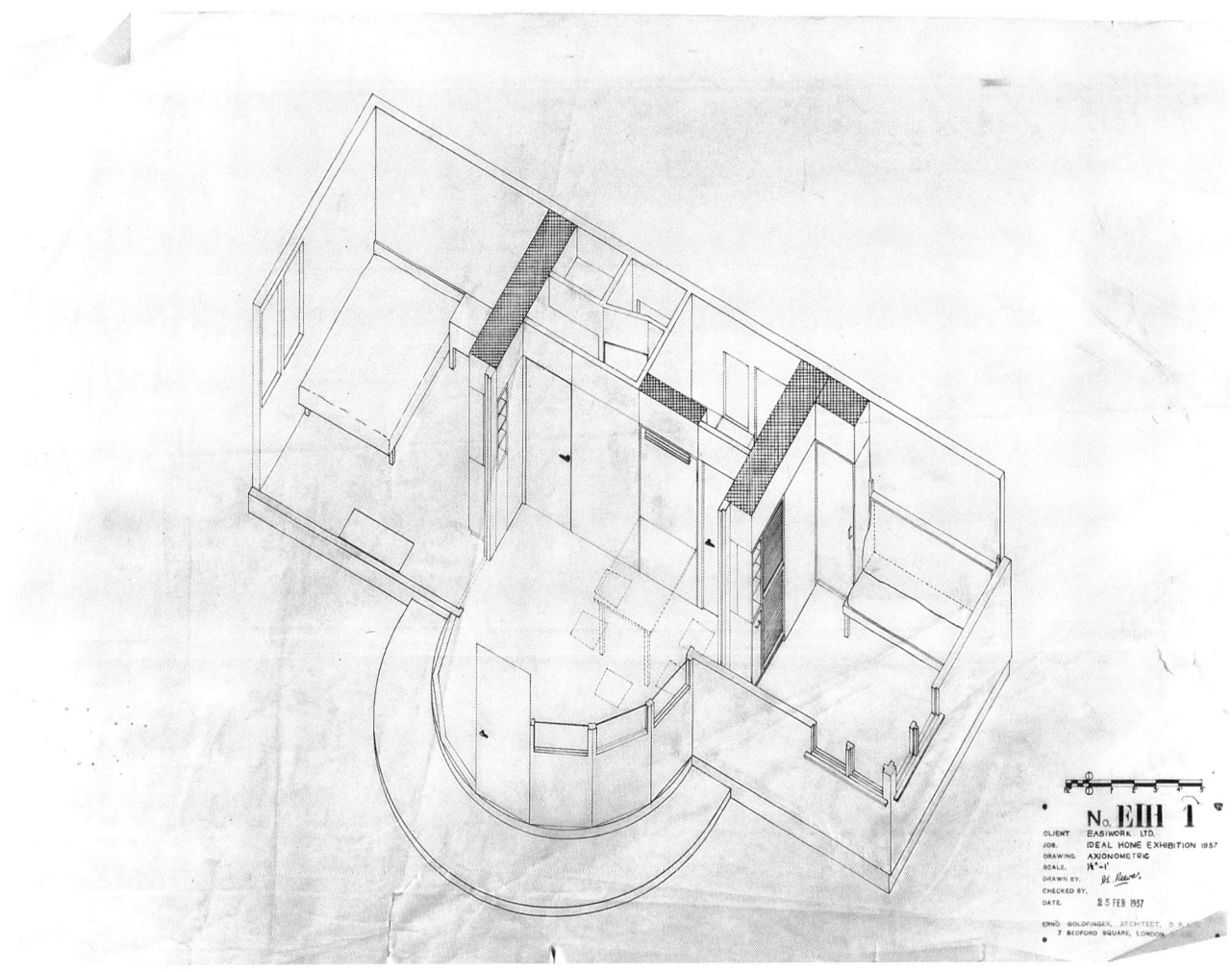

28. Design for display stand for Easiwork furniture, Ideal Home Exhibition, Olympia, London, 1937

Drawn by David L Reeves. Pen on tracing paper (505 × 810)

The 'All-In' Bungalow, which was to be manufactured by the Norwich firm of Boulton & Paul, was claimed to be a new departure in homes for 'the week-ender, the pensionnaire and all those who appreciate the many advantages of inexpensive living accommodation' as it came fully fitted out with furniture specially made for its three rooms. This furniture was Goldfinger and Easiwork's EFE, now re-named Architecto Unit Furniture, and its waxed oak units, making use where possible of rolling shutter fronts, were intended to be hygienic and labour-saving. The general tone of the furnishing 'considered on needs and not tradition' was described as 'restrained modernism' and an interesting feature of the bungalow was the way in which, for the sake of compactness, cupboard units were used to subdivide it into separate rooms. This strategem was repeated in the house at Broxted.

29. Design for children's section in the British Pavilion for the 1937 Exposition Internationale des Arts et Techniques dans la Vie Moderne, Paris, 1936

Pencil, charcoal and coloured crayon on backed tracing paper (315 × 505)

Goldfinger was asked to design the children's section in conjunction with the Abbatts by Oliver Hill who was in overall charge of the British Pavilion. The section formed part of the larger exhibit of the Weekend House which included a living room designed by Gordon Russell and a kitchen by Mrs Darcy Braddell. Although the executed design differed from this drawing, its strong sense of fun and imaginative spirit remained, its stylised cut-out clouds and artfully assembled displays of model boats and other toys providing welcome relief from the *Country Life* view of Britain with its emphasis on sport, wealth and 'le weekend' presented elsewhere in the pavilion.

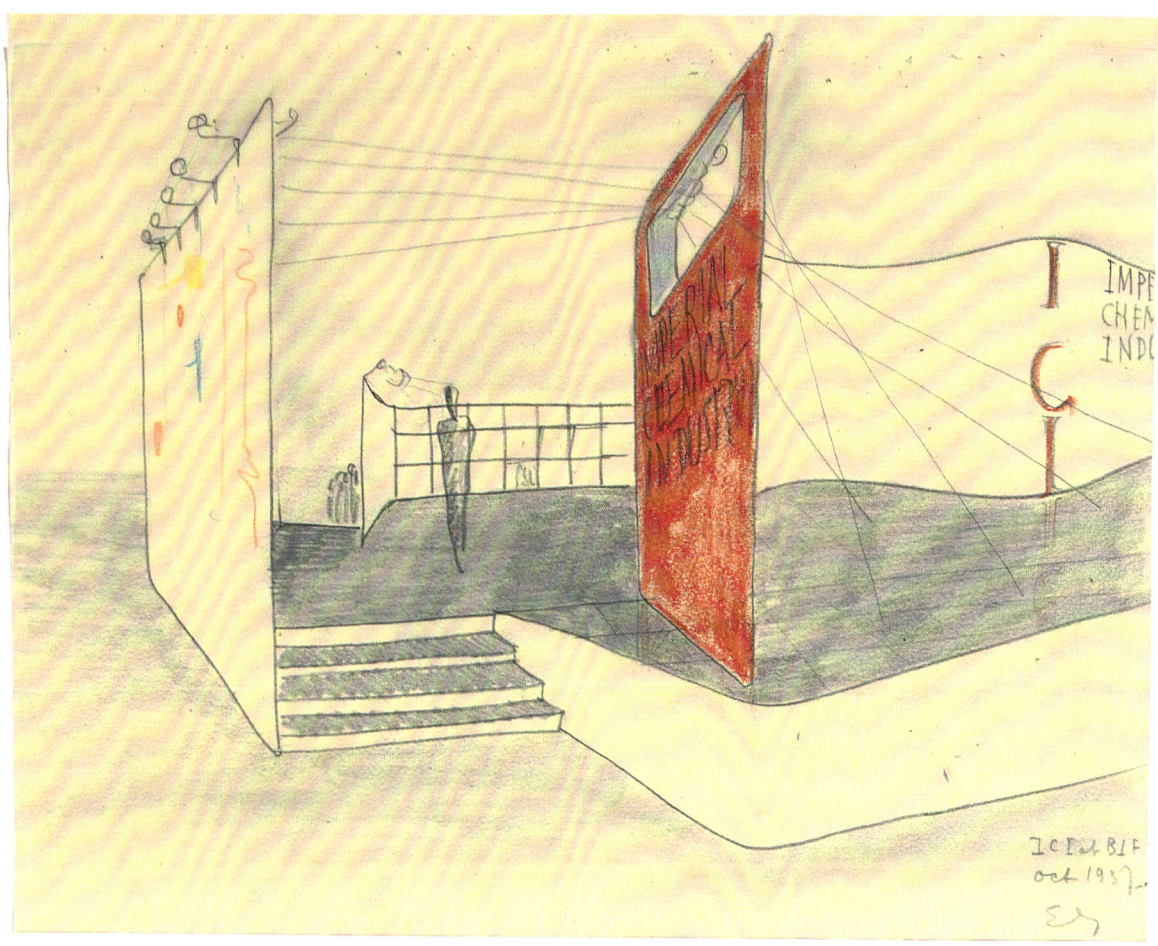

30. Design for ICI stand at the 1938 British Industries Fair, Olympia, London, 1937

Pencil and coloured crayon on tracing paper (210 × 265)

This stand inaugurated a new policy by ICI to exhibit each year at the British Industries Fair the production of one of its component companies. In this case the focus was on alkali products and the stand was designed as far as possible using materials derived from such products, including galvanized iron, glass bricks and Vitroflex.

The correspondent of the *Architects' Journal* was impressed by the colourful display which related the history of alkali beneath a canvas canopy supported by three steel masts: 'It really throbbed with the life of charged wires, moving wheels and running water, and is . . . one of the most brilliant pieces of display design I have seen.'

31. Design for exterior, 1-3 Willow Road, Hampstead, London, *c* 1938

Pen and pencil and brown and blue washes (315 × 505)

The plans drawn up by Goldfinger and Flower for this terrace of three houses sparked strident protests from members of the Hampstead Heath and Old Hampstead Protection Society led by the future Home Secretary, Henry Brooke, who mistakenly believed that the architects were proposing 'a "modern" angular house in reinforced concrete' which would be 'disastrously out of keeping' with the character of the neighbourhood. Goldfinger, supported by other local residents, including Flora Robson and Roland Penrose, trenchantly defended the houses: 'They are designed in a modern adaptation of the eighteenth-century style, and are far more in keeping with the beautiful Downshire Hill houses round the corner than their neighbours in Willow Road ... As for the objection that the houses are rectangular, only the Eskimos and Zulus build anything but rectangular houses.' Far from being examples of 'white box' Modernism the houses are of reinforced concrete frame with red brick facing, the horizontality of their beautifully proportioned elevation emphasised by the combination of the three houses into a single terrace thereby cleverly disguising the real height of the building which can only be properly appreciated from the rear. Ironically 2 Willow Road was formally handed over to the National Trust by the Heritage Secretary, Peter Brooke, son of the scheme's most voluble opponent.

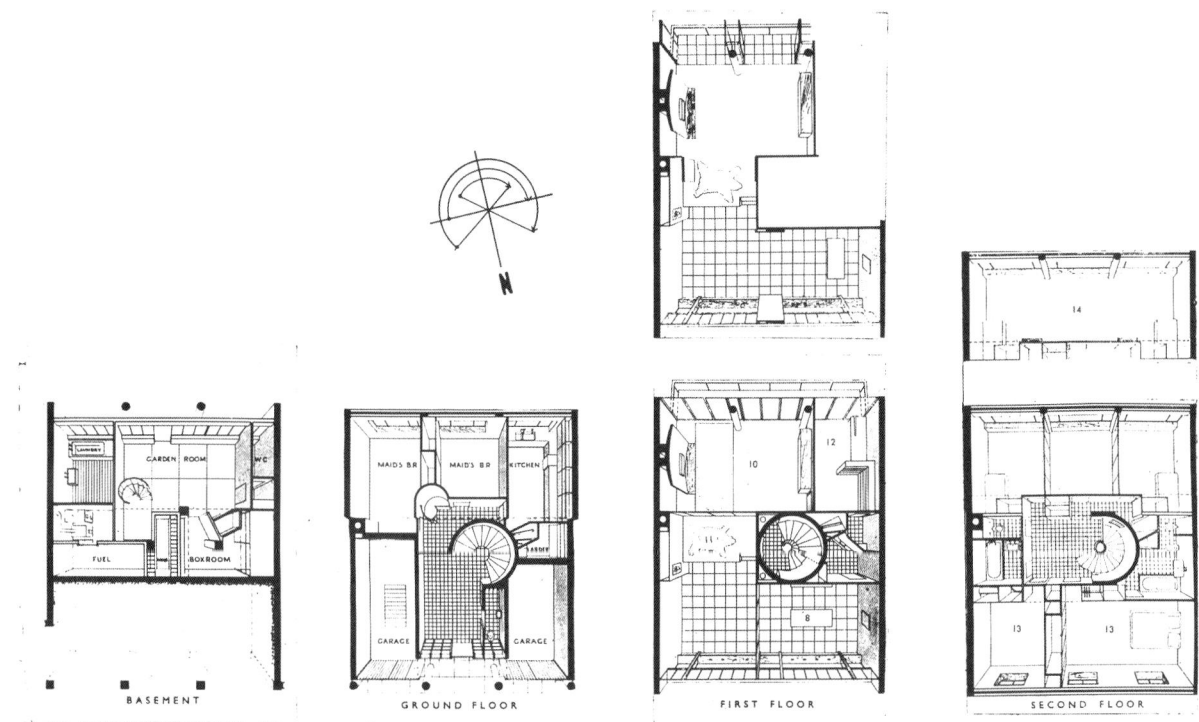

32. Drawings made for publication of 2 Willow Road, Hampstead, London, 1940

Print (445 × 565)

The three houses each had a different plan. The middle one, the largest, was built for Goldfinger's own use, the other two helping to finance the scheme. Goldfinger later described the plan thus: 'No corridors! A hierarchy of spaces with the utmost plan economy. It was designed to be adaptable. Walls could – and have been – moved.' These effects were achieved by the reinforced concrete frame, which enabled the creation within of large uninterrupted areas, and by the ingenious deployment of the spiral staircase which was the only fixed point in the house and which occupied the barest minimum of space. The staircase freed the living quarters on the first floor and the children's rooms above to radiate round it in a free-flowing fashion. Thus all the rooms on the first floor, except the study, together with the three nurseries on the second, were only divided by sliding partitions which could be folded back to create one large room or other intriguing variations in scale and space.

33. Design for interior of 3 Willow Road, Hampstead, London, 1938
Pencil on tracing paper (265 × 375)

The chaste symmetry of the facade of the Willow Road block masks free-flowing interiors with strategically placed concealed lighting enhancing the dramatic spatial effects after dark. Number three, though smaller than number two, was similar in its interior treatment. In Goldfinger's own house the walls are mainly lined in waxed oak and most of the furniture and fittings were designed by Goldfinger himself. They reveal his close attention to detail – the light switches and door handles, for example, are all lined up at a convenient stomach level. The steps of the spiral staircase are similarly carefully graduated in height and the substitution of balusters by rope threaded through loops in bronze rails imparts a nautical air typical of other Modernist works of the period. Although the interior is distinguished by its clean lines and minimum of ornament, the art works (many now sadly dispersed) which Goldfinger had collected from his early days in Paris when he was on intimate terms with, among others, Braque and Léger, were used, together with books, plants, cushion covers, etc, to introduce a note of vivid colour. The large windows of number three, shown here, with deep sills for the display of art objects, project over the entrance and afford fine views of the heath. Above them, at transom level, Goldfinger's photobolic screen, designed to reflect light deep into the interior, is used for the first time.

34. Design for alterations to 13 West Hill, Highgate, London, for Andrew Wordsworth, 1939

Pen, coloured washes, turquoise pastel, blue and brown gouache on board (555 × 810)

This drawing, not as executed, shows a raised fireplace area and extensive use of wood panelling similar to the design for the *Ideal* *Home* bungalow two years later. Easiwork furniture and Goldfinger's characteristic uplighters also formed part of the design.

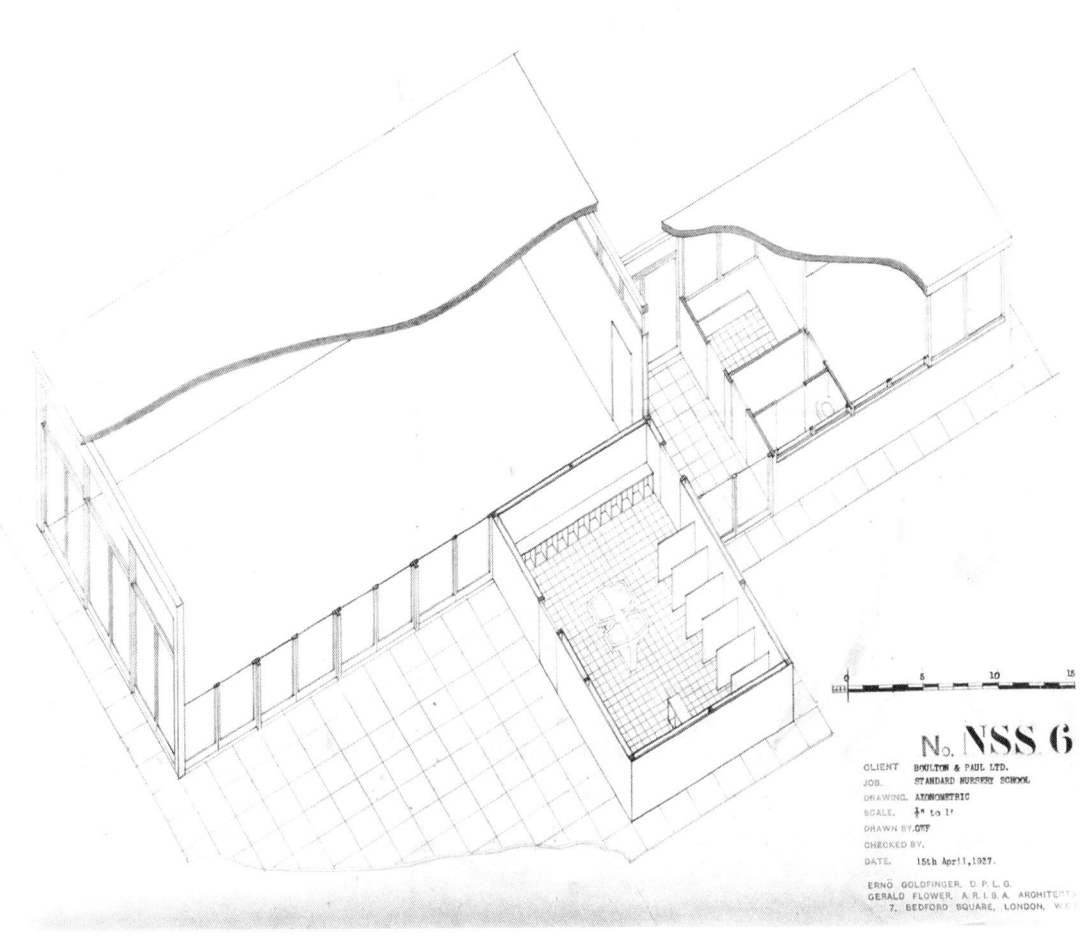

No. **NSS 6**

CLIENT   BOULTON & PAUL LTD.
JOB.   STANDARD NURSERY SCHOOL
DRAWING. AXONOMETRIC
SCALE.   ¾" to 1'
DRAWN BY.GWF
CHECKED BY.
DATE.   15th April,1937.

ERNÖ GOLDFINGER, D. P. L. G.
GERALD FLOWER, A. R. I. B. A. ARCHITECTS
7, BEDFORD SQUARE, LONDON, W.C.

35. Design for a standard nursery school for Boulton & Paul Ltd, 1937

Drawn by Gerald W Flower. Pencil on tracing paper (400 × 465)

In 1937-38 Goldfinger refined the ideas explored in his expanding nursery school in a series of further designs drawn up with his partner, Gerald Flower, and Mary Crowley, who was later to become one of the prime movers in the pioneering post-war school building programme in Hertfordshire. To a modest degree these designs employing prefabricated standard elements presaged that programme. Although wood was little used as a structural material during this period the exemption of schools from the building bye-laws and the desire of educationalists for buildings of a more temporary nature rendered it an increasingly attractive option. This school, therefore, was composed of easily transportable standardised timber sections with weatherboarding on the outside and plywood within. If an extension was required additional units could simply be bolted on. Although Boulton & Paul, its prospective manufacturers, received a number of enquiries and it was estimated that the school could be supplied at a cost of £25 per child, it was never marketed.

Ideal Home
magazine   aug 1941

36. Drawing made for publication of *Ideal Home* bungalow, 1941

Pen on tracing paper (200 × 295)

This design by Goldfinger and Mary Crowley was published in *Ideal Home* in October 1941 as part of a series called 'Planning for the Future' which began in February of that year and continued through thirty instalments until August 1943. The series aimed to stimulate constructive thought about the problems of replanning once the war was over and included contributions from FRS Yorke, Judith Ledeboer and Elizabeth Denby. Goldfinger and Crowley's single-storey house was designed for a family with two children and the living room shown here had large windows separated by plain brick piers opening onto a south-west facing terrace. The area around the fireplace at the far end of the room was raised up to give a feel of greater intimacy and the wall behind was wood panelled. The accompanying article took the form of an imaginary conversation between a visitor and the bungalow owner whose verdict was that: 'it is certainly much nicer to live in and very much easier to run than the mock Tudor house we used to rent'.

DUPLEX DORMITORY FOR 6 CHILDREN

ENTRANCE TO COMMUNAL BLOCK

HOLIDAY & EVACUATION CAMP FOR FAMILIES II

37. Design for holiday and evacuation camp for families for the AASTA Evacuation Committee, 1940

Print with pencil and coloured crayon added (1020 × 750)

As war loomed evacuation became a pressing problem. The government scheme, which by 1940 had built forty camps under the aegis of the National Camps Corporation to a design by Thomas Tait, came under increasing attack for its waste and disorganisation, especially from the Evacuation Committee of the Association of Architects, Surveyors and Technical Assistants of which Goldfinger was a member. In 1940 Goldfinger and Mary Crowley with the help of Anne Parker presented their own alternative ideas for five different types of camp accommodation in a Camps exhibition held at the Abbatts' shop in Wimpole Street. This drew on the designs formulated by Goldfinger, Crowley and Justin Blanco White which had won second place in the Building Centre's School and Holiday Camp Competition of 1939. The approach adopted in the exhibition made use of suitably dispersed and camouflaged prefabricated timber units and emphasised the importance of long-term planning over short-term expediency. The designs thus attempted to integrate the camps more thoroughly with the surrounding neighbourhood and to provide for alternative uses in peacetime. They also paid particular attention to the needs of mothers and young children under five which the government had ignored.

38. Design for London Women's Parliament exhibition, Boots, Piccadilly Circus, London, 1943
Pen and coloured washes on backed tracing paper (265 × 380)

The London Women's Parliament was set up in 1941 to stimulate discussion of women's problems and to achieve a better deal for women through parliamentary action. It issued 'bills' on matters such as housing and health and reports like *You CAN Get a War-time Nursery in your District.* Ursula Goldfinger played a prominent role in its affairs and the Parliament's exhibition at Boots in Piccadilly Circus, the main theme of which was to 'make women more conscious in their responsibilities and opportunities', was designed by Ernö. Through a series of photographs, drawings and graphs the exhibition told the story of two Mrs Britains, represented in reality by two London clippies, the one, whose hopes for a better future after the First World War had been dashed by unemployment and the rise of Fascism, and the other, her politically active daughter-in-law whose vigorous campaigning and greater involvement in all aspects of life would ensure the fruits of victory would not again be squandered.

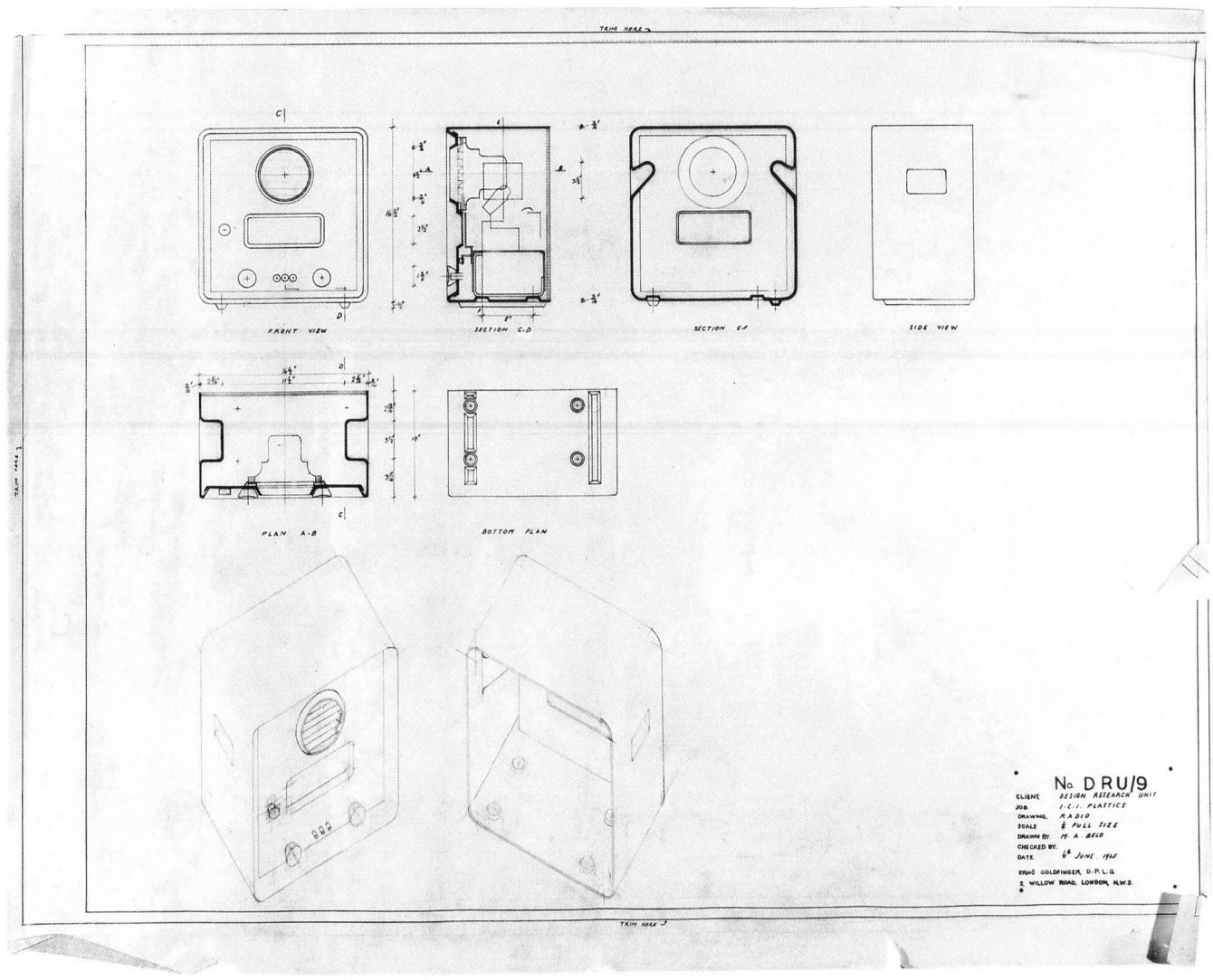

39. Design for a radio in perspex for the Design Research Unit, 1945

Pencil on tracing paper (320 × 425)

In 1944 the Design Research Unit, which had been set up in the previous year and whose members included Misha Black, Sadie Speight and Milner Gray, was engaged by ICI to investigate the possible uses of perspex. At that time perspex was still a relatively new material having first been developed by ICI in 1935 and the intention was to design a series of objects and then have demonstration prototypes made. Goldfinger was approached by Frederick Gibberd, another DRU member, in December 1944 to submit designs for a number of items, among them a fluorescent light fixture, a chair, kitchen utensils and this radio. Although Goldfinger's architect colleagues in the MARS Group, Serge Chermayeff and Wells Coates, had designed radios in plastic for Ekco before the war which were subsequently marketed, neither this design nor any of the others were developed and ICI terminated its contract with the DRU in August 1946.

40. Design for *The Cinema* exhibition, for the Army Bureau of Current Affairs, 1943

Charcoal on detail paper (400 × 505)

During the war years Goldfinger produced a number of exhibitions for the Army Bureau of Current Affairs (ABCA) on subjects such as the *LCC Plan for London* and *Health Centres*. The ABCA had been set up in 1943 as part of the more general Army Education Scheme in the belief that the better informed soldier would be a better fighter. Through the 120 exhibitions it organised each year it not only played a key role in disseminating knowledge of current affairs to the men at the front but also in fostering their expectations of a better world to come once the war was over. About ten copies of each exhibition were sent to the army command for distribution to individual units. The exhibitions were designed to a standard format – 20 by 15 inch panels on linen-backed cartridge – so that they could be easily transported in wooden boxes on the backs of motorbikes to isolated units. To capture the attention of soldiers drained by the demands of war it was important that the information contained in each was presented in as straightforward but visually striking a manner as possible.

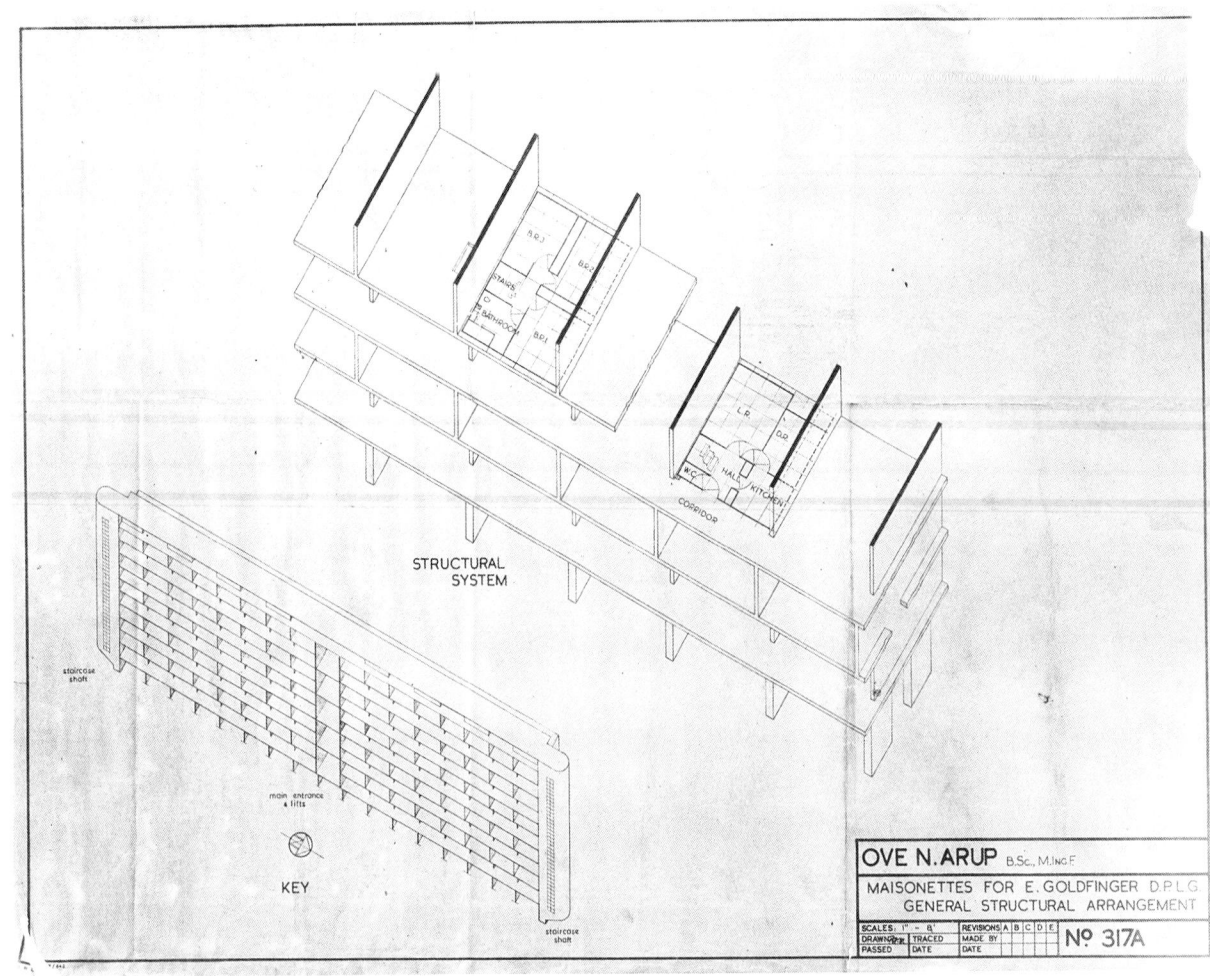

STRUCTURAL
SYSTEM

staircase
shaft

main entrance
& lifts

KEY

staircase
shaft

OVE N.ARUP B.Sc., M.Inc.F.

MAISONETTES FOR E. GOLDFINGER D.P.L.G.
GENERAL STRUCTURAL ARRANGEMENT

SCALES: 1" = 8'	REVISIONS A B C D E	
DRAWN BY	TRACED	MADE BY	№. 317A
PASSED	DATE	DATE	

41. Engineers' drawing prepared by Ove N Arup for box-frame housing, *c*1944
Print (530 × 685)

To prepare for post-war reconstruction Goldfinger spent the war years investigating the possibilities for mass housing, partly in collaboration with the engineer, Ove Arup. In 1941 Arup had issued a pamphlet entitled *Safe Housing in Wartime* which advocated the building of bomb-proof hostels using innovative methods of box-frame construction. Not only could these hostels later serve as dwellings but they would also eliminate the need to erect costly separate shelters which would be redundant as soon as the war was over. As shown by his evacuation camp projects, Goldfinger also believed in building for long-term use rather than simply to meet emergency wartime requirements. Arup's original proposals had only envisaged blocks of up to five storeys but with Goldfinger's help designs were prepared for much taller schemes. These were promoted in Arup's 1944 *Memorandum on Box Frame Construction for Terrace Houses and Flats* and Goldfinger's large post-war housing blocks were built using box-frame methods.

42. Drawing showing a typical modern type of urban enclosure, 1942

Print with coloured washes added (330 × 490)

This drawing was reproduced in Goldfinger's article, 'The Elements of Enclosed Space', published in *The Architectural Review*, and subsequently in the *Ideal Home* series 'Planning for the Future'. It illustrated how future multi-storey housing units, built according to the box-frame system, could be grouped compactly but far enough apart not to overshadow each other or to allow neighbours to peer in. Relying as it did on the distinct separation of solid structural elements – internal dividing walls, floor and roof which were combined to form the frame – and their non-structural counterparts, such as external walls or further partitions, the box-frame system was especially suited to flat construction and made it possible, as here, to provide large window areas. Although tentative experiments with box-framing had been made during the 1930s, particularly by Burnet Tait & Lorne in their Evelyn Court, Hackney (1935), it really came into its own after the war when it was found to facilitate rational site organisation and large-scale production, as well as permitting non-structural elements to be prefabricated in the dry, all of which were factors of crucial importance in tackling the chronic housing shortage.

TRAFFIC

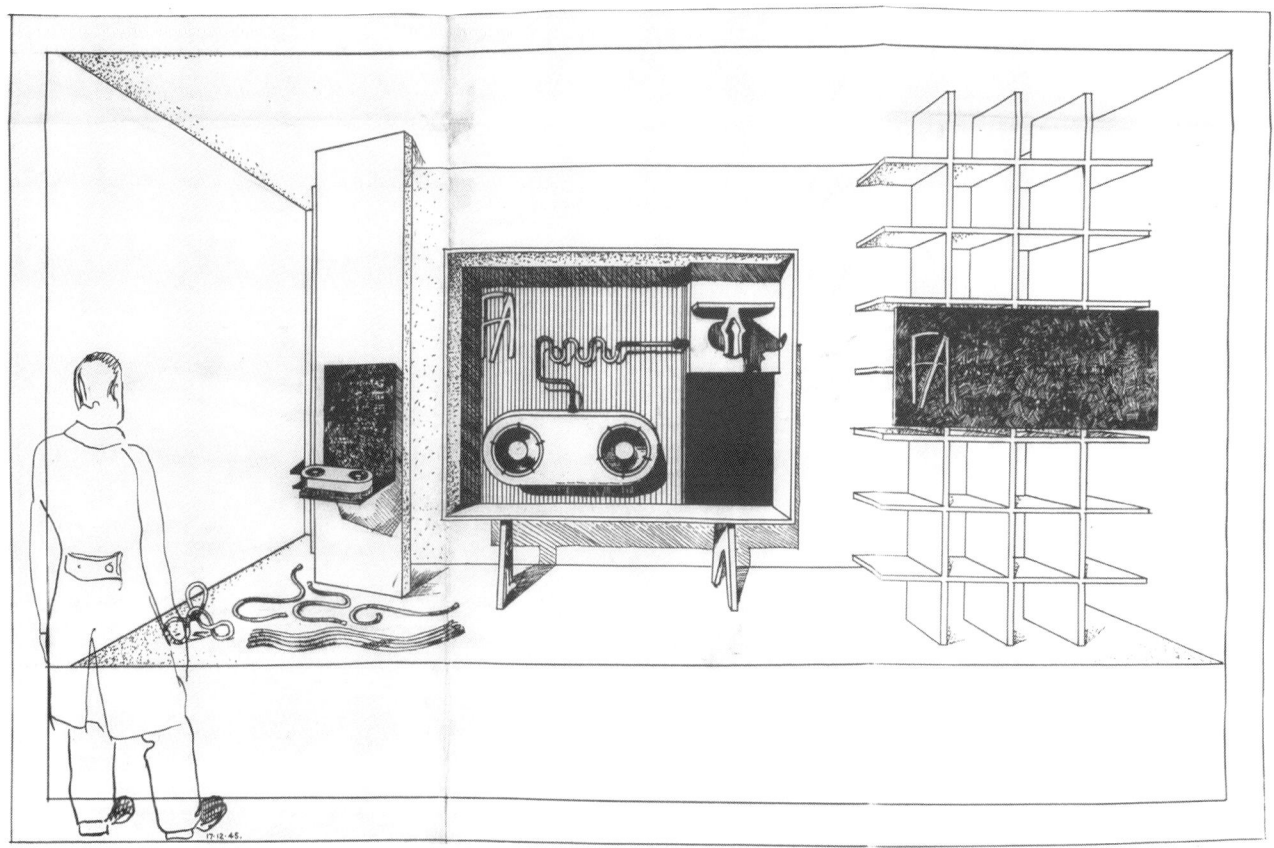

43. Design for *Traffic* exhibition, for the Army Bureau of Current Affairs, 1944

Pen and charcoal on detail paper (700 × 520)

Intended to highlight the inefficiency of traffic crossings, this drawing underlined one of Goldfinger's most strongly held tenets of social planning, namely the strict separation of pedestrians and traffic. The drawing was reproduced again in his *County of London Plan Explained* (1945), written with EJ Carter, where Goldfinger discussed Sir Patrick Abercrombie's plan for London and revealed his own vision for the city which was heavily influenced by Le Corbusier. Goldfinger thus advocated the restriction of through traffic to a series of parkways with local traffic passing over or under these roads and able to join them only at lengthy intervals. Traffic crossings would be rendered redundant and the main social units of home, work and play would be separated from the main arteries by generous bands of open space given over to parks, playing fields and allotments. Similarly, the smaller social units of the neighbourhoods would be kept free of anything but the purely domestic traffic of its inhabitants so that 'no young child will ever have to cross a main road on his way to school'. Goldfinger's concern with traffic, therefore, was part of a much wider belief in the virtues of compact planning and the CIAM maxims of 'soleil, espace, verdure'.

44. Design for exhibition display for Friedman & Athill, 1945

Pen on tracing paper (280 × 465)

Goldfinger designed stands for Friedman & Athill, manufacturers of Neat Gas Appliances, for exhibitions at the Building Centre in Glasgow (1946) and in London (1948). This naive but vigorous drawing is very much in the style of those for the ABCA.

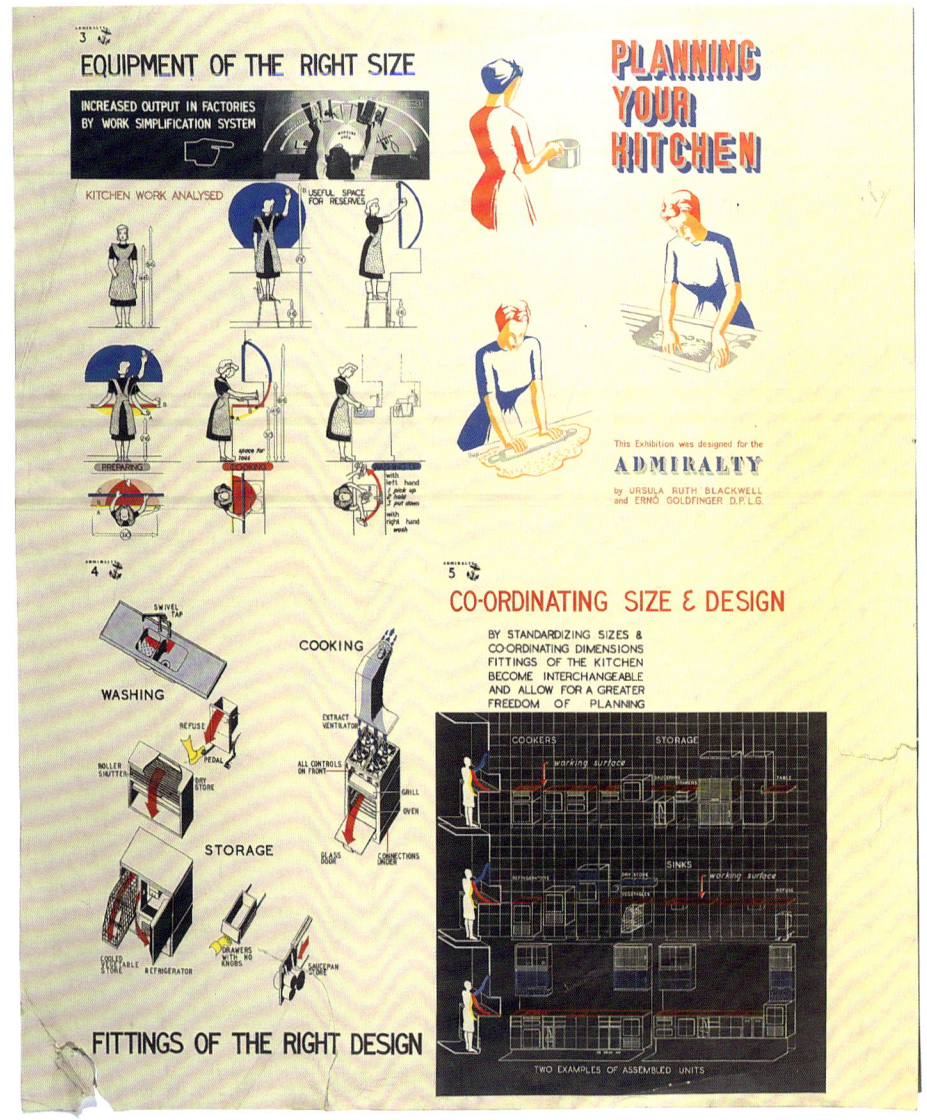

45. Design for *Planning Your Kitchen* exhibition, for the Admiralty, 1944

Print (775 × 650)

Goldfinger's involvement in kitchen design and his concern for ergonomics, evident in his pre-war projects for Easiwork, continued in wartime with schemes for the *Reynolds News* Ideal Kitchen (1944) and this for the Admiralty. Both schemes stressed the importance of simple, well-designed equipment so arranged as to facilitate an easy sequence of tasks. Using interchangeable standardised units the kitchen was thus compactly planned to keep to-and-froing to a minimum and particular attention was paid to ensuring that worktops were at a convenient height to eliminate unnecessary fatigue through constant bending – ideas which at the time had been realised more fully in the United States than here. The exhibition panels were subsequently used as part of a housecraft training scheme.

46. Design for prefabricated housing project for the Association of Building Technicians, 1945

Print with coloured crayon added (360 × 245)

This drawing showing the erection of prefabricated houses was used as the cover of *Prefabricated Homes*, a pamphlet written by Bernard Cox and published for the Association of Building Technicians in 1945. With a foreword by Sir Charles Reilly it advocated prefabrication as the only feasible way to tackle the chronic housing shortage, Cox arguing that the traditional policy of building homes to last as long as possible had resulted in slums, that houses should be regarded as 'consumer instead of capital goods', and their lifespan restricted to a period of thirty years. All this was anathema to Goldfinger who adamantly opposed temporary building because it resembled 'the commercial methods used in the motor car and wireless industries, by which consumption of luxury articles was artificially fostered (by making last year's model look out-of-date). As long as by means of standardisation we can build more lasting, better equipped and cheaper houses, it is in the interests of the community that it should proceed – But if it is to serve the long-term profiteering of industry by producing dwellings of limited life, then it should be considered as a social danger.'

47. Exhibition panel, *Planning Your Neighbourhood*, for the Air Ministry Directorate of Educational Services, 1945

Print (490 × 370)

Compiled with the assistance of Ursula Blackwell and Peter Shepheard and using the striking cartoons of Sheila Hawkins this is a good example of the simple graphic style used in wartime exhibitions to put the message across to the soldiers – in this case how a bombed area of Shoreditch could be rebuilt according to the precepts of the County of London Plan with Goldfinger again stressing the importance of maintaining closely knit neighbourhoods. These exhibitions achieved a wide circulation as, although in the first instance they were prepared for the ABCA, it was usual practice for other ministries and the British Council to order further sets.

48. Design for the *Daily Worker*, 75 Farringdon Road, London, for Peoples Printing Press Ltd, 1946

Drawn by Martin L Cobbett. Pencil on tracing paper (375 × 510)

The brief was to transform a bomb-damaged Victorian warehouse into a modern newspaper building and the plan was dictated by the thorough analysis Goldfinger and his partner, Colin Penn, made of the methods of newspaper production. The original intention had been simply to convert the existing building and to provide it with a new entrance, as shown here, but in the end a substantial rebuilding from the first floor up was found to be essential. The engineer on this work, Goldfinger's first large-scale commission, was Felix Samuely, one of his colleagues from the MARS Group and a member of the Design Research Unit. The building has been demolished.

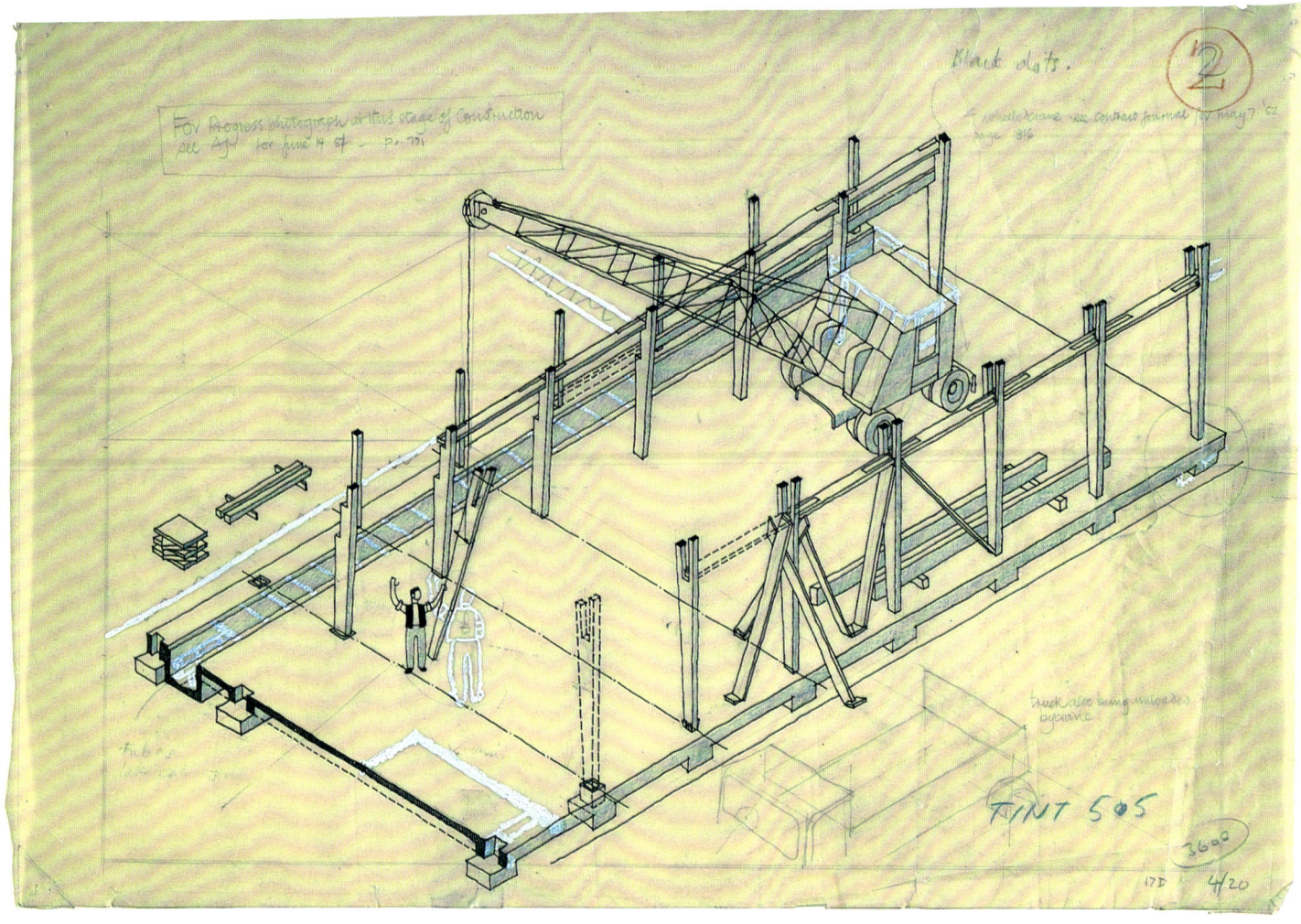

49. Drawing of prefabricated construction system for schools for London County Council, 1950

Pen, pencil, blue crayon and Chinese white on tracing paper (300 × 430)

Commissioned by the London County Council to build two schools, at Brandlehow Road, Wandsworth, and Westville Road, Hammersmith, Goldfinger devised his own prefabricated concrete system for use in both. Its main advantage was speed of erection with only twenty-four days, four men and a two-ton mobile crane needed to put up the frames. The crane also enabled a smaller number of heavier and more economical units to be used and both schools were built well below the limit of £170 per place set by the Ministry of Education. The drawing shows part of the construction process. The crane moved across a reinforced concrete platform, dropping the columns into holes where they were wedged temporarily in an upright position. The crane then helped to position beams onto the column ledges and the bracing units were fixed into their grooves. Permanent assembly then began with the lintels and sills being used as distance pieces and the columns being secured to the beams and lintels by joints cast *in situ*.

KIOSK
FESTIVAL OF BRITAIN
ERNŐ GOLDFINGER ARCHITECT
69-70 PICCADILLY LONDON W1

1951

50. Design for a kiosk for the Festival of Britain, South Bank, London, 1951
Drawn by DM. Pen on tracing paper (560 × 505)

Goldfinger's involvement in the Festival was slight. His plans for a series of telephone booths, some of them doorless, were shelved after objections from the Post Office which insisted that all the boxes should be properly sound-proofed. The only examples of his work on the site were sixteen vending kiosks for ice cream, tobacco, official publications and souvenirs which, said Hugh Casson in a letter to Goldfinger, were 'greatly admired'. In contrast Goldfinger's pre-war assistants, Ralph Tubbs and HT Cadbury-Brown, designed such major structures at the Festival as the Dome of Discovery and the Land of Britain Pavilion.

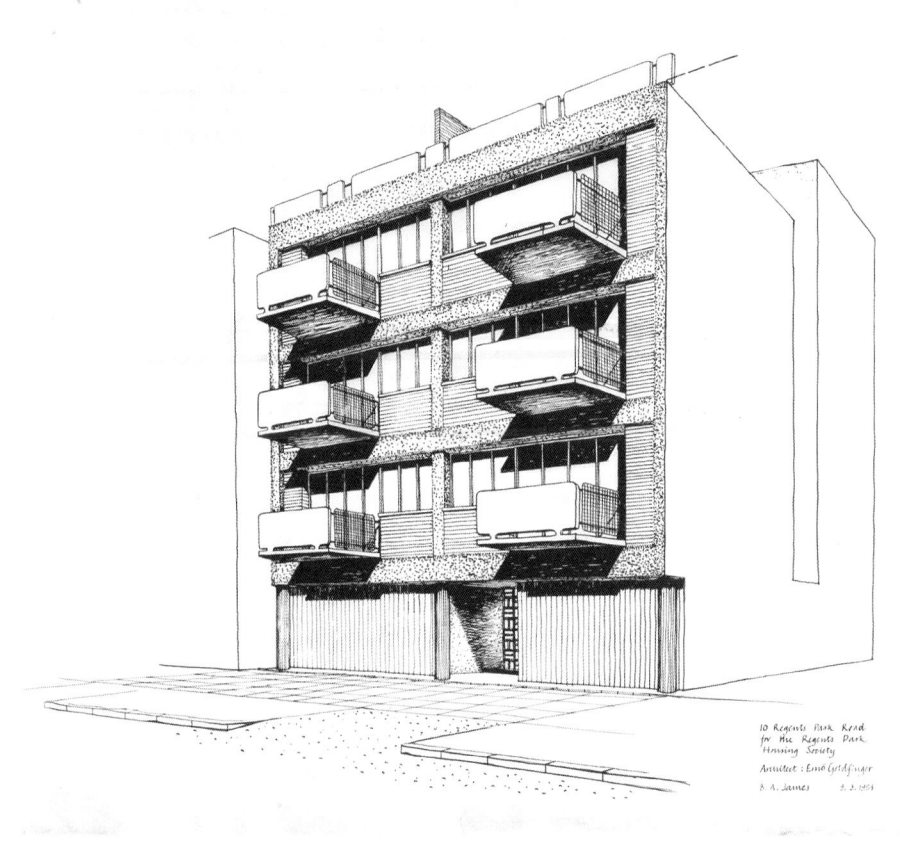

In the drawing: *10 Regents Park Road for the Regents Park Housing Society. Architect : Erno Goldfinger. B. A. James 9.3.1954*

51. Design for a block of flats, 10 Regent's Park Road, London, for the Regent's Park Housing Society, 1954

Drawn by BA James. Pen on tracing paper (465 × 500)

This scheme aroused much interest as it was a joint building venture of a kind popular in post-war Sweden and Denmark but rarely seen in Britain mainly because of high land costs, stringent building regulations, and the possibility of legal wrangles. In 1952 ten families formed themselves into the Regent's Park Housing Society to build their own homes and were thereby able, under the terms of the 1936 Housing Act, to acquire a 90 per cent mortgage at a favourable rate. They purchased a bomb-damaged site in a terrace of early nineteenth-century stucco houses. Planning regulations obliged Goldfinger to respect the cornice line of the original terrace although he was able to include a recessed fourth storey. The reinforced concrete frame itself formed many of the flat's internal divisions and, following proposals he had made in the ABCA exhibition *Planning Your Home* (1946), the dining area could either be incorporated into the living room or the kitchen. While elements of the design, particularly the treatment of the ground floor, look back to Willow Road, the projecting concrete balconies prefigure Goldfinger's later work. By the time the flats were eventually completed in 1956 many of the original members of the Society had sold their shares.

52. Design for offices for Carr & Co, Cranmore Boulevard, Shirley, Birmingham, 1955
Pen and pencil on tracing paper (570 × 945)

This office block was designed as a free-standing prestige building next to the company's paper factory. Austere and rational, it has a number of characteristics in common with Albemarle Street: it was planned on Goldfinger's 2-foot 9-inch grid; the main elevation clearly expresses its reinforced concrete frame; and photobolic screens are employed to increase daylight penetration of the building. The main offices are on the first and second floors carried on pilotis above the open ground floor reception area permitting, Goldfinger wrote to his client, 'that spatial organisation which you may have admired on the Continent'. An earlier scheme envisaged the use of precast stone cladding but the final design was of reinforced concrete in a variety of finishes – exposed aggregate, bush hammered, and *béton brut*. A typical Goldfinger spiral staircase abuts the north elevation and the roofscape is dominated by a large tower which houses the plant and a document store. Described by Pevsner as 'impressively clear and crisp' it has been recommended for listing by English Heritage.

53. Design for 45-46 Albemarle Street, London, for Albemarle Street Properties Ltd and Mason Pearson, 1955

Print with pencil added on tracing paper (710 × 510)

With the cooperation of the individual owners Goldfinger was able to treat this scheme, actually for two buildings, as one unified design, which, said *The Times*, 'repays close study as an exact modern equivalent of 18th century street architecture'. Each building is self-contained but the second and fourth floor bay windows, though divided by a thin mullion, stretch across both acting as a strong unifying element – an aspect of the design attacked by more dogmatic critics for upsetting the Modernist credo that the elevation should reflect the layout of the interior. The offices, now listed Grade II, were widely praised at the time for conforming to the scale of their eighteenth-century neighbours and the rhythm of the street, not least by Lewis Mumford in the *New Yorker*. 'Here is a building that has not merely learned the lessons of modern form but has learned them thoroughly enough to feel free to learn, too – from the eighteenth century and the Regency – how to create a lively facade for a street that must be modernized. Here the past has been neither externally imitated nor crassly rejected but inwardly absorbed and recreated . . .'

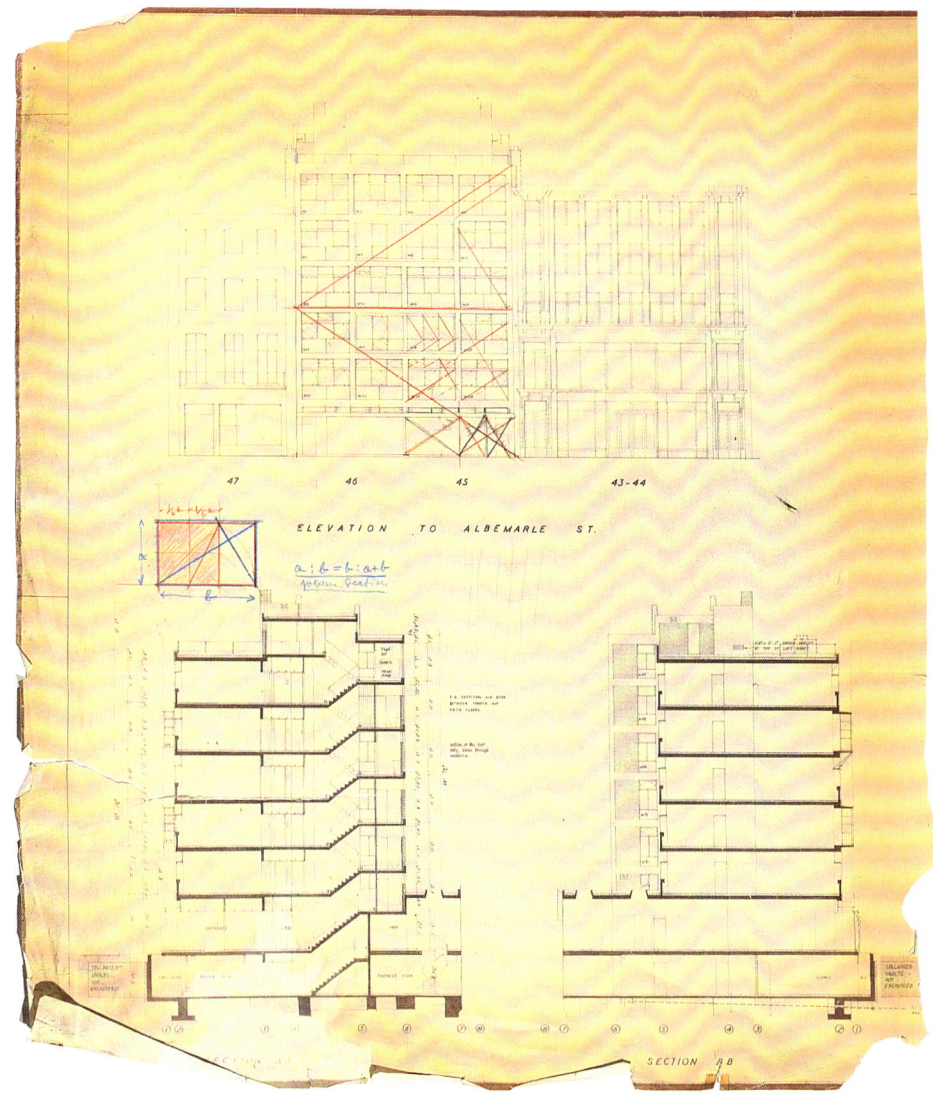

54. Contract drawing for 45-46 Albemarle Street, London, for Albemarle Street Properties Ltd and Mason Pearson, 1955

Drawn by John Roberts. Print with red and blue crayon and pencil added (730 × 1015)

As this illustration demonstrates, the proportions of the facade were determined by Goldfinger's use of the Golden Section about which he wrote: 'I design all my buildings on a proportion derived from the Square (Golden Section or $\sqrt{2}$, $\sqrt{3}$, $\sqrt{4}$, etc) and use a rigorous control of the elements of facades and plans. The plans are also controlled by a grid of 2 ft 9 in (giving 5 ft 6 in, 8 ft 3 in, 11 ft as multiples and 1 ft 10 in, 11 in or 3 in increments). This gives me control of scale.' This emphasis on symmetry was a legacy of Goldfinger's Beaux-Arts training.

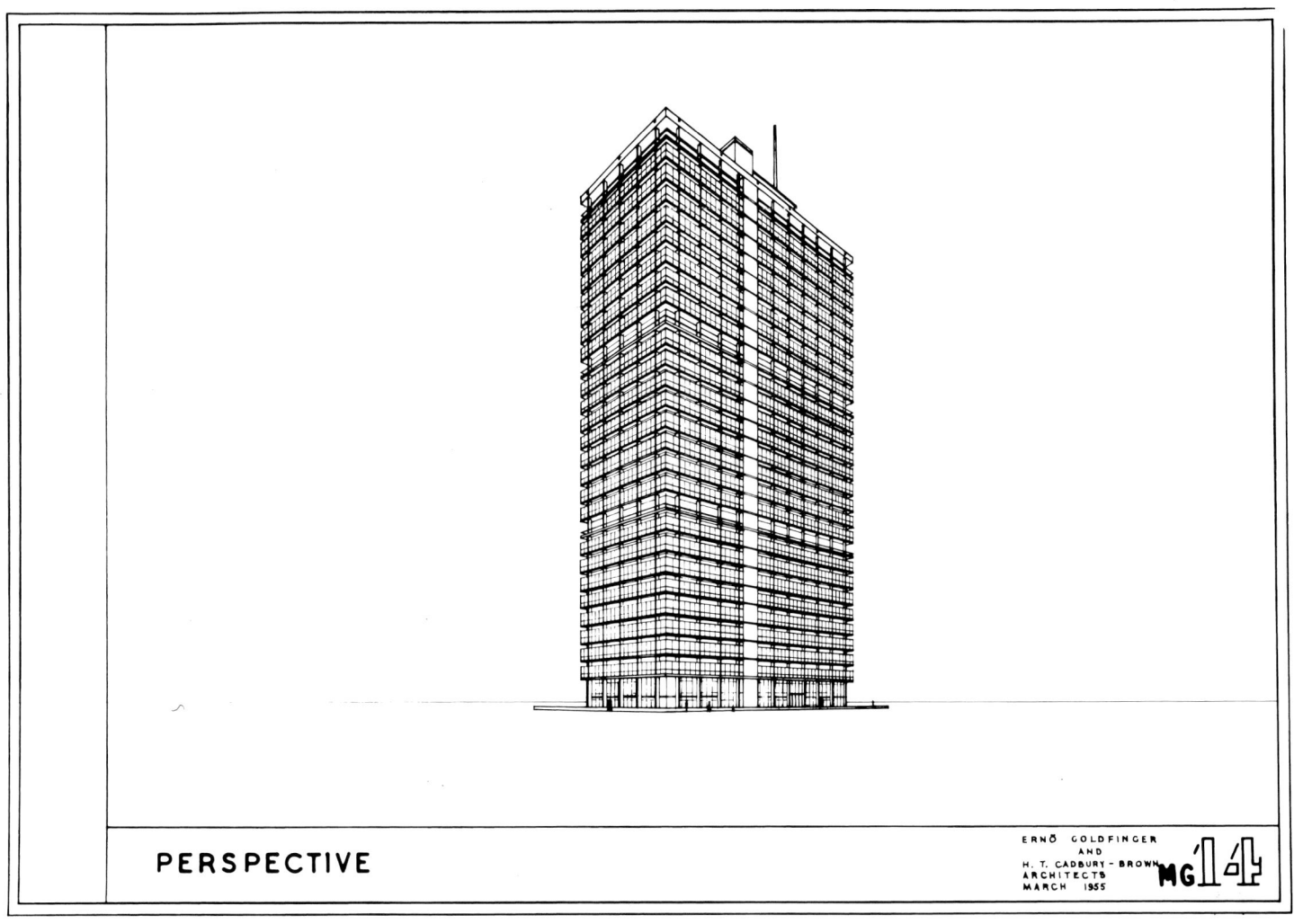

PERSPECTIVE

ERNÖ GOLDFINGER
AND
H. T. CADBURY-BROWN
ARCHITECTS
MARCH 1955 MG 14

55. Design for office skyscraper, Moorgate, London, 1955

Pen on tracing paper (400 × 575)

This project with HT Cadbury-Brown for a 27-storey block on the site now occupied by BP was a design exercise to investigate the economics of tall buildings. The lifts were ingeniously arranged in a central core and two side shafts, stopping at the ninth and eighteenth floors, to maximise lettable space. Externally these lift interchange floors were expressed by a balcony running round the building which gave modulation to its facade and helped relate it to its nine-storey neighbours. Describing the design Goldfinger rejected as inappropriate the approach adopted by Mies van der Rohe in his influential

Seagram Building, New York, under construction at the time: 'The facade has been developed in depth both from the functional point of view and also to give richness of light and dark to the whole building. It was felt that this building has to relate to a surrounding scale which is considerably lower than itself, unlike cities in America where the tall buildings create and exist in their own scale. The shiny hard and glittering box was not considered to fulfil the requirements of character for such a building in the City of London. A greyness and depth and interest in profile was considered of more importance.'

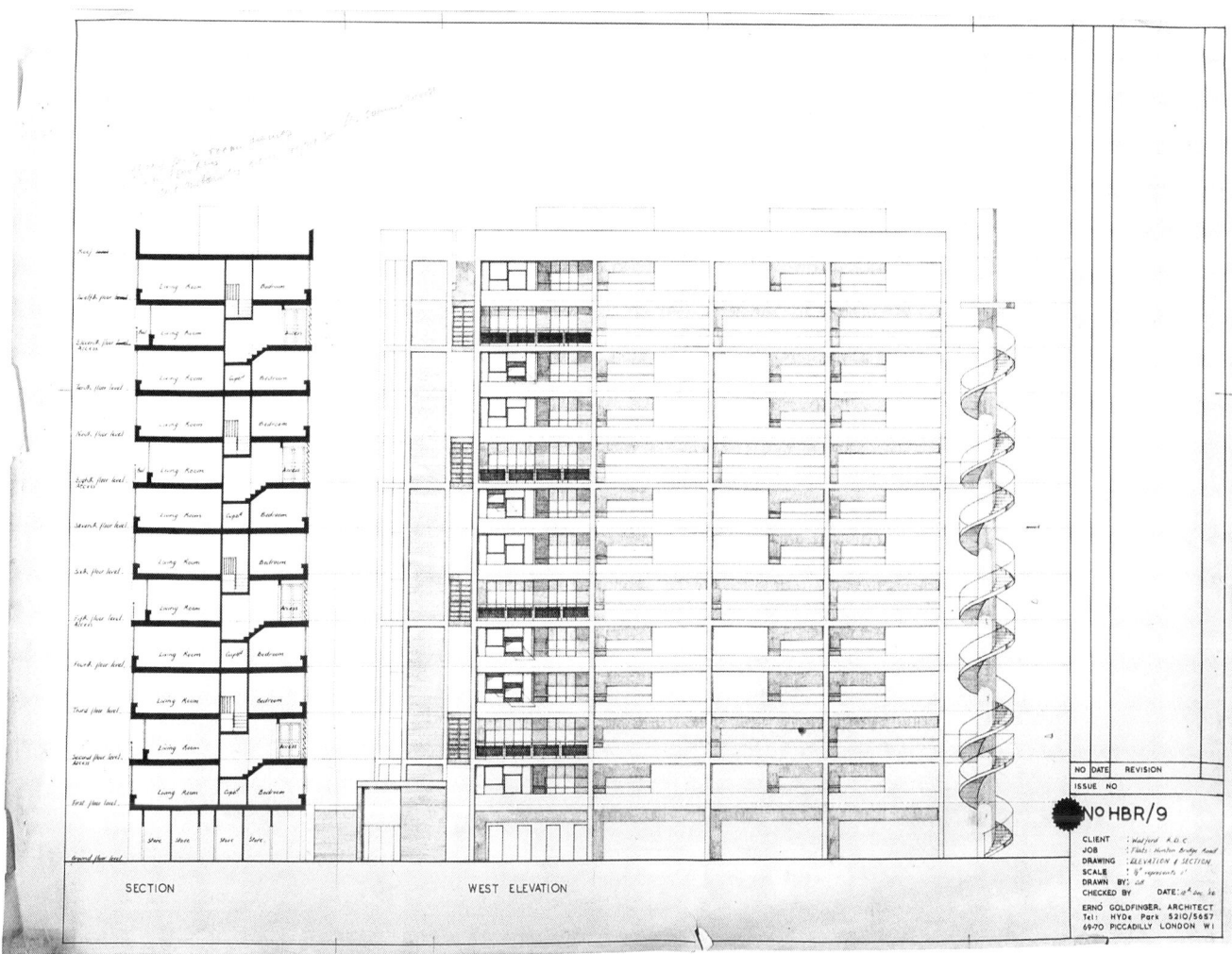

SECTION   WEST ELEVATION

56. Design for housing, Hunton Bridge Road, Abbots Langley, for Watford Rural District Council, 1956
Drawn by DB. Print (560 × 760)

Goldfinger's insistence that dwellings should be concentrated in order to interfere as little as possible with the surrounding landscape found expression in his first local authority housing commission. His proposal for a compact nine-storey block which would have allowed the retention of adjoining trees and parkland was, however, rejected by the local authority as ugly and out of harmony with the rural surroundings – criticisms which Goldfinger countered by asserting: 'They do everything to get rid of the rural surroundings. They make them a sprawling suburb.' The scheme as finally completed in 1961 was indeed far looser consisting of twenty-eight dwellings arranged in three separate blocks. This preliminary design, however, shows Goldfinger formulating for the first time the idea of an enclosed access gallery on every third floor which was to be repeated in later housing schemes.

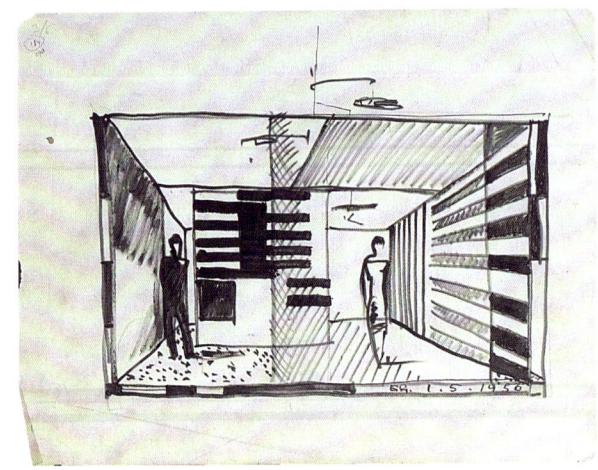
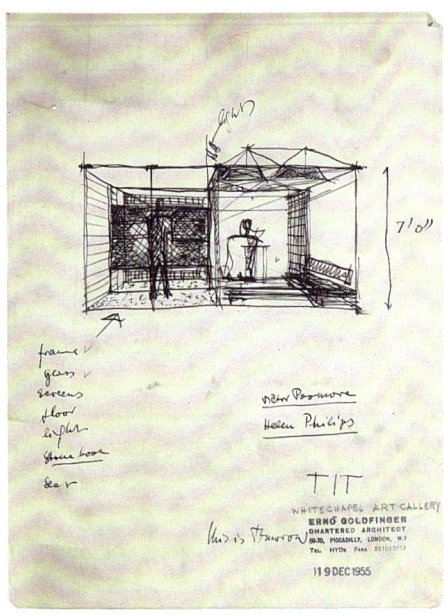
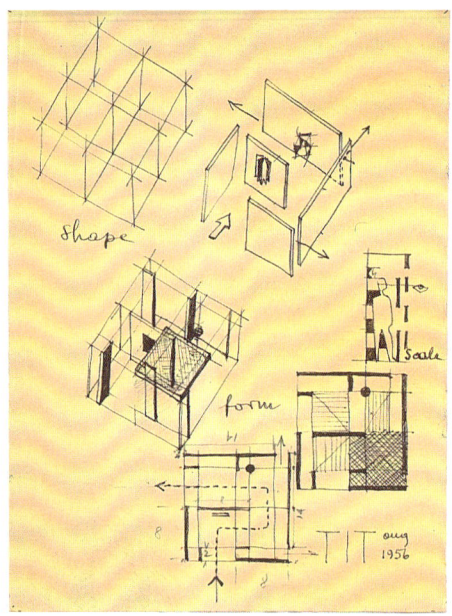

57. Preliminary studies for *This Is Tomorrow* exhibition, Whitechapel Art Gallery, London, 1955-56
Print with yellow, red and blue crayon added (210 × 285); pen on tracing paper (215 × 280); pen on tracing paper (280 × 215); print (280 × 215)

This well publicised and attended show, opened by Robbie the Robot, consisted of twelve exhibits each designed by a team comprising an architect, painter and sculptor, most of whom had been former members of the English *Groupe Espace*. The aim was to explore the common ground between art and architecture. Critics considered the exhibitors fell into two distinct groups which they labelled the Independents and the Constructivists. The former stressed 'the relationship between onlooker and the world at large rather than between him and the qualities of a work of art. The work is significant as a symbol, not a form.' The latter brought 'sculpture and architecture together in genuine synthesis. These works aspire to an ideal style, a conscious purity of form.' The exhibit of Goldfinger and his partners, the artist, Victor Pasmore, and the sculptor, Helen Philips – a refined cube with colourful reliefs and a hanging balsa wood sculpture – was highly praised and regarded by Basil Taylor in the *Spectator* as 'the most mature, confident and persuasive example of the constructivist ideal of co-partnership'. Most attention, however, was focused on the patio and pavilion exhibit of the Smithsons, Nigel Henderson and Eduardo Paolozzi, a 'garden shed' of aluminium, corrugated plastic, rusting bicycle wheels and other domestic junk.

58. Design for a house in the Vale of Health, Hampstead, London, for Dr Hemans, 1958
Print with pencil and coloured crayon added (475 × 710)

This rerun of the Willow Road saga encompassed moments of farce and a burning issue of the time – the exercise of planning controls by unqualified individuals. Goldfinger's design for a new house on the site of the Victorian Athenaeum which for a time had acted as a workshop for the Old Vic was opposed by Hampstead Borough Council on grounds of aesthetics and density. Its spokesman, engineering assistant WJ Grove, declared: 'I think this development would look all right on its own in a thickly wooded setting – possibly in Scandinavia.' John Summerson, supporting Goldfinger, argued that the Victorian villas in the Vale 'were about as low as English archi-tecture had ever sunk' and that Goldfinger 'was a very good archi-tect at the rigorous end of the modern idiom; his was a very good building, a plain statement, clean in design and would give some sort of definition to that part of Hampstead.' Despite a favourable report, the Minister of Housing, none other than Goldfinger's old Willow Road adversary Henry Brooke, took four months to approve the scheme by which time Goldfinger's client had moved else-where. An indignant *Architects' Journal* seethed: 'It is this kind of thing that is bringing planning into disrepute and discouraging modern architecture.'

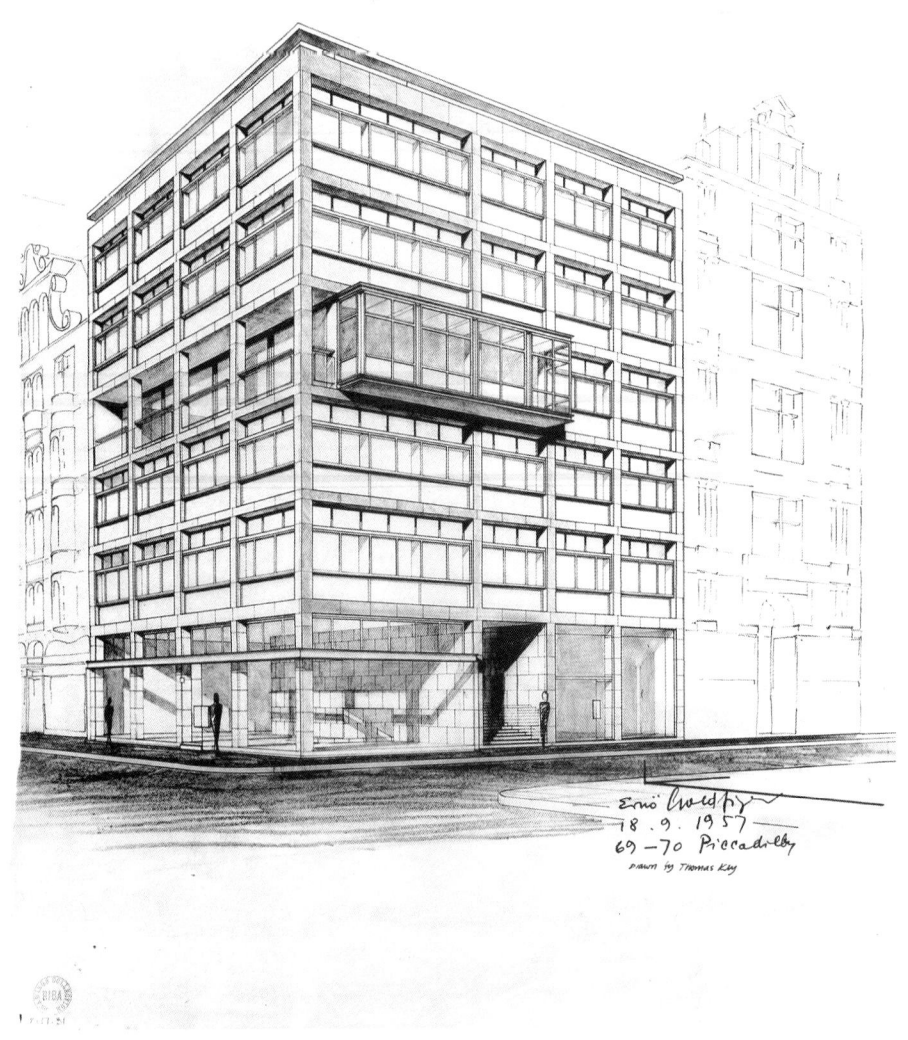

59. Design for office building, 69-70 Piccadilly, London, 1956

Drawn by Thomas Kay. Pen and pencil on tracing paper (560 × 490)

This projected redevelopment of the building in which Goldfinger had his office almost forms a pair with his nearby Albemarle Street scheme. The treatment of the facade is very similar although here the cladding material is grey granite rather than Portland stone and the design has been adapted to the requirements of a corner site. The site was eventually developed by another architect in 1972.

60. Design for Hille House, Watford, for S Hille & Co, 1959

Print with pencil and pen added on tracing paper (630 × 920)

This reinforced concrete three-storey block fronting the main St Albans road was part of a four-stage development carried out by Goldfinger for Hille, the furniture manufacturers. The block contained offices and showrooms for Hille as well as additional offices and shops for rent. A feature of the facade was its precast concrete block window filled with brightly coloured glass which hid the main executive office. This decorative device, which was similar to that employed by Le Corbusier at the Unité d'Habitation, Marseilles (1952), was used on numerous occasions by Goldfinger, for example, at the Elephant and Castle and most notably in his Vale of Health house where it formed the major exterior decorative element.

61. Design for Alexander Fleming House, Elephant and Castle, London, for Imry Properties Ltd, 1959
Print with pencil, pen and Chinese white added on tracing paper (710 × 860)

Various ideas to improve traffic circulation at the Elephant had been proposed since the beginning of the century but it was not until the County of London Plan (1943) that they took substantive shape. Abercrombie's proposal for a polygonal road junction and major shopping centre was further developed by the London County Council in the early 1950s when the Elephant was designated a comprehensive development area. In 1956 the Council issued a brochure setting out its ideas for a dumbbell shaped traffic intersection and inviting designs for offices and shops on the five sites it owned. Goldfinger and his developer client, Imry Properties Ltd, were successful in the subsequent competition for Site 2 with their scheme for Alexander Fleming House, viewed here from the north-west. The Elephant that finally emerged, a hostile environment set amidst a cluster of towers with no central focus and pedestrians condemned to a labyrinthine network of subways, was, however, very different to what the LCC had intended. Commercial imperatives and the failure to acquire all the sites were partly to blame, but above all the two essentially contrasting visions of the Elephant as both a major gateway into London and an important shopping centre, the one implying transience, the other a place to linger, were never satisfactorily resolved.

62. Design for Alexander Fleming House, Elephant and Castle, London, for Imry Properties Ltd, c 1959

Drawn by J Blacker. Print (780 × 1210)

Ignoring calls by the LCC that the site should be perimeter planned, Goldfinger's scheme instead consisted of three freestanding blocks, two of seven storeys and one of eighteen, grouped around a central piazza. The old Trocadero cinema enclosed the piazza on the remaining side. At the same time Goldfinger also published proposals for the layout of the entire area in similar vein culminating in a tall Y-shaped tower at its northern end. Perretesque in its detailing, Constructivist in its massing, Alexander Fleming House developed the themes first articulated at Albemarle Street with alternating projecting bays and recessed balconies used to give variety and modulation to the boldly expressed concrete frame. As at the time the exact use of the building was unclear, Goldfinger provided open decks which could be readily subdivided and lighting and electrical arrangements were made as flexible as possible. 'The essence of modern building', wrote Goldfinger, 'is to provide a permanent frame with the interpolation of less permanent membranes and a system of services . . . which can be added or subtracted at will'.

63. Preliminary studies for block D, Alexander Fleming House, Elephant and Castle, London, for Imry Properties Ltd, 1962
Pen and coloured washes on detail paper (250 × 375)

The Ministry of Health chose Goldfinger's buildings for its new headquarters and two additional blocks, D and E, were added making it one of the largest office complexes in the country. This sketch, characteristically vigorous, shows the massing of the blocks and the pushing and pulling of the facade of block D. The recipient of a Civic Trust award in 1964, Alexander Fleming House has since been at the centre of fierce controversy sparked by its owners' proposals for recladding. To some a grim reminder of the worst of 1960s 'grey concrete monoliths', to others 'a major example of the Constructivist ethic', it was the most surprising omission from English Heritage's roll of post-war buildings worthy of consideration for listing.

64. Competition design for a shopping centre at the Elephant and Castle, London, for Imry Properties Ltd, 1960

Drawn by Hugh Cannings. Print with mixed media including collage added on board (585 × 1220)

This competition entry for shops and offices on Site 1 at the Elephant was one of the five (out of thirty-six original submissions) short-listed for further consideration. It was ultimately unsuccessful, the winners being Boissevain & Osmond with a galleria-type shopping centre. Goldfinger's design was carefully arranged to fit in with Alexander Fleming House in order to form an integrated townscape. The two office blocks it envisaged were planned on the same 16-foot 6-inch grid and the facades, though treated individually to avoid monotony, were in general very similar. The shopping centre itself was distinguished by its use of highly coloured and strategically placed advertisements as an integral part of the composition in a manner that was at once both reminiscent of Russian Constructivism of the 1920s and in tune with 1960s Pop Art.

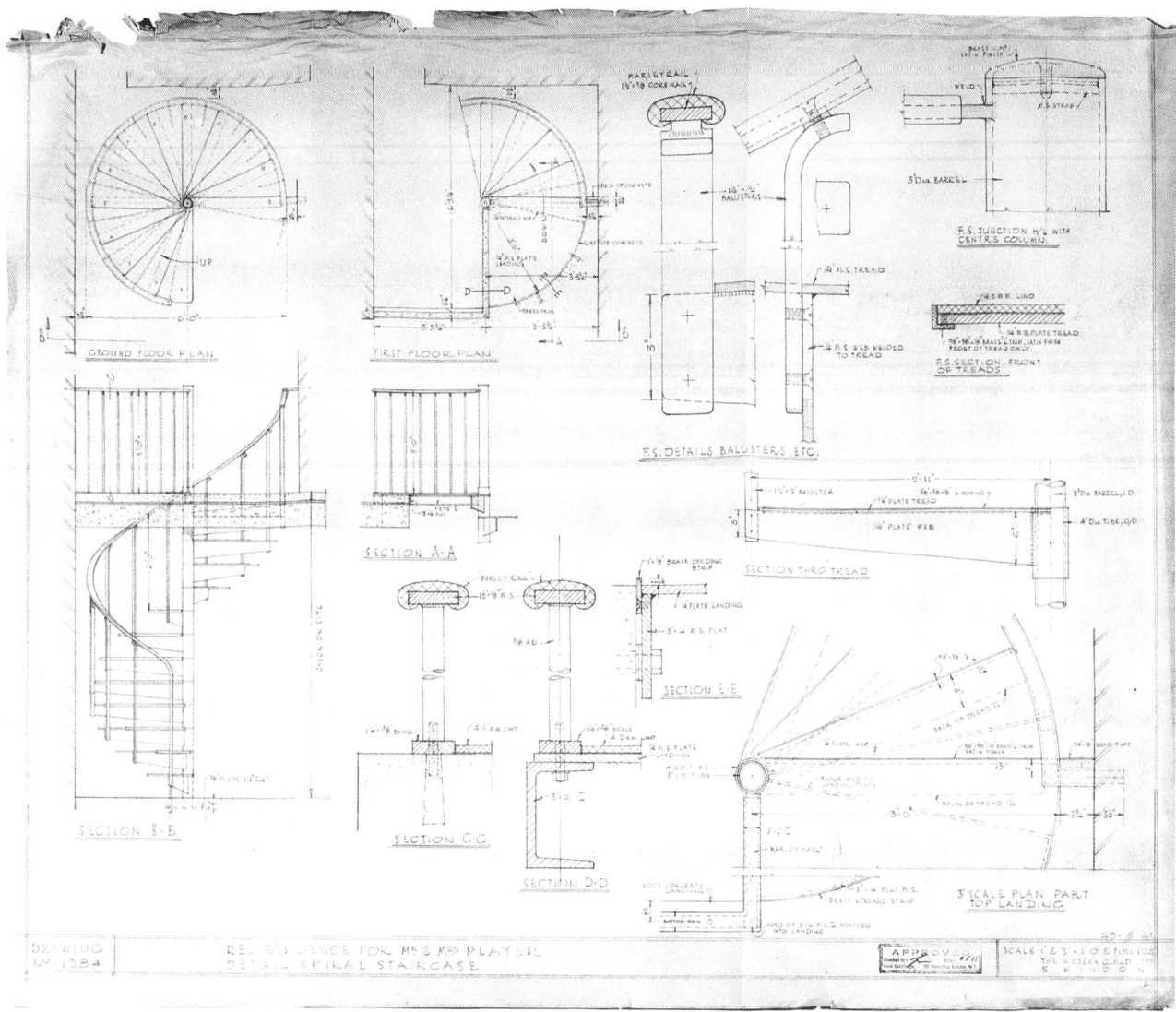

65. Working drawing for spiral staircase, Lime Tree House, Combe Hill Road, Malden, Surrey, for Mr and Mrs Player, 1961
Print (715 × 870)

After living with the Goldfingers at Willow Road for two years when she was a child, Lucy Player wished to have a similar house built for herself. Built of brick with precast concrete floors her house was a rather ascetic Modernist structure. The main living accommodation, as at Willow Road, was on the first floor and was reached by a steel spiral staircase with white lino treads and a handrail of plastic-covered metal. The owners died soon after the house was completed and although superficial alterations were later made it still survives relatively intact. At the time of writing, however, it is threatened with demolition.

66. Presentation drawing of office development, Bloomsbury Square, London, for Hammerson Properties Ltd, 1962

Drawn by Gordon Cullen. Pen, pencil and pastel on tracing paper (475 × 600)

Despite being an admirer of Georgian architecture, Goldfinger drew up this design for the property developers, Hammerson, which would have entailed the demolition of several listed eighteenth-century houses in Southampton Place. Goldfinger later defended his proposal, a mixed development of offices, shops and flats, the chief feature of which was a 350-foot high slab block intended to provide a visual counterpoint to Charles Holden's Senate House, by explaining: 'Bloomsbury – I like that gridiron system. I thought it justified to create a pivot and put a very tall block on the axis of Bloomsbury Square as a pivot with a chaos behind. I believe in axes.' At the ensuing public enquiry the scheme was supported by Lionel Brett, Nikolaus Pevsner and James Richards, editor of *The Architectural Review*, all of whom agreed with Goldfinger's contention that as Southampton Place was not a complete street and that 'streets with teeth missing are not convincing' its demolition was justified. Despite Pevsner's opinion that the proposed design was 'of greater importance in the whole pattern of mid-twentieth century London than the houses in Southampton Place can ever have been within the pattern of their time' it was turned down.

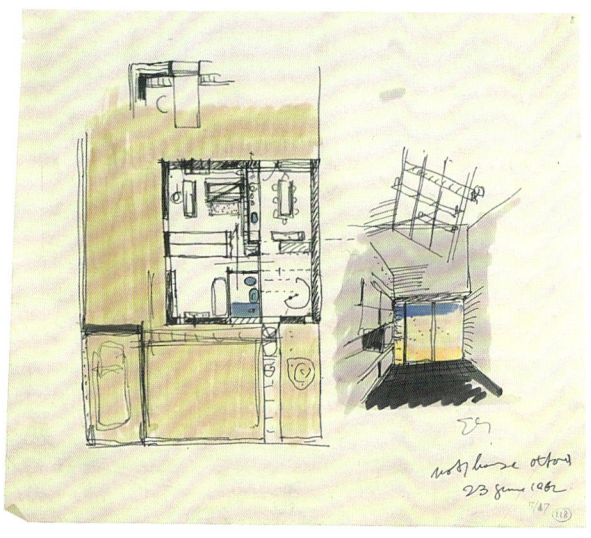

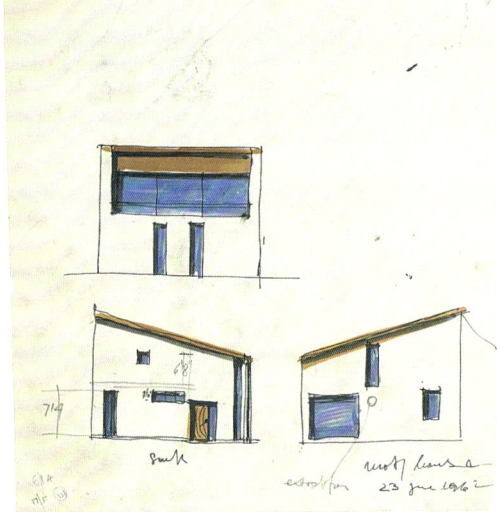

67. Preliminary designs for house, Bedford Street, Oxford, for Mr and Mrs H Motz, 1962

Pen, pencil and coloured washes on tracing paper (250 × 430; 250 × 300; 250 × 245)

These vividly coloured impressionistic sketches exploring initial design ideas are typical of Goldfinger's working methods. Later more formal drawings would be worked up by assistants under his strict supervision. The Motz house was a compact brick dwelling with similarities in treatment to The Outlook at Le Touquet, particularly in its use of a monopitch roof.

68. Design for Odeon, Elephant and Castle, London, for Fortpost Investments Ltd and Rank Organisation Theatre Division, 1965

Pencil, pastel and red pen on detail paper (415 × 590)

Although the competition was admittedly thin, the Odeon, Elephant and Castle, was generally considered to have been the country's best post-war cinema. It was also something of a rarity at the time in that it was designed as a freestanding cinema rather than being subsumed within a larger complex – witness the near contemporary Odeon, Marble Arch, which is almost completely hidden beneath a tall office block. The cinema replaced George Coles's massive Trocadero (1930) and shows how cinema decoration had changed over thirty years, Cole's ornate Italian Renaissance extravaganza giving way to Goldfinger's stark functionalism. Despite a chorus of protests, the cinema was demolished by its owners, Imry Merchant Developers, in 1988, its spokesman maintaining: 'I thought it could have been designed by the people who designed Hitler's concrete bunker'.

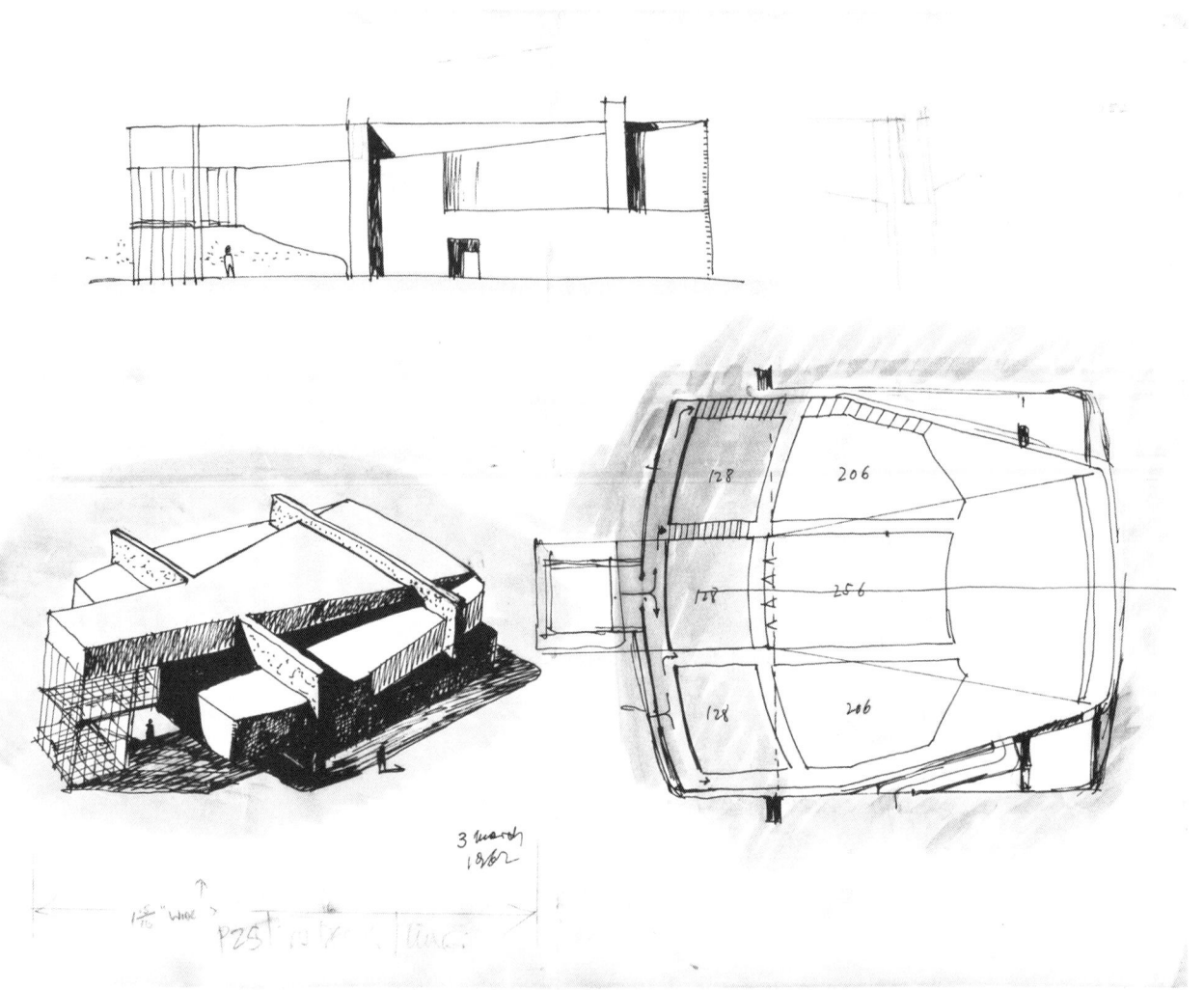

69. Design for Odeon, Elephant and Castle, London, for Fortpost Investments Ltd and Rank Organisation Theatre Division, 1962

Pen, yellow wash and red gouache on tracing paper (380 × 560)

The sculptural shape of the concrete exterior, likened to a crouching beast, represented an unusual departure from the normally rectilinear nature of Goldfinger's work and was a frank expression of the cinema's internal volumes and of its adroit structural arrangement. Two diagonal concrete beams, attached at one end to the perimeter wall and at the other to a massive post-tensioned beam slung across the auditorium, carried the auditorium's roof whilst also reflecting its sight lines and the arc of the cinema projector. These beams, which were clearly visible on the outside, internally gave the impression that the projection booth was hovering perilously in space. The booth was also expressed externally and embellished with Odeon lettering. Here at last, wrote Reyner Banham, was 'a cinema that is not a castrated theatre'.

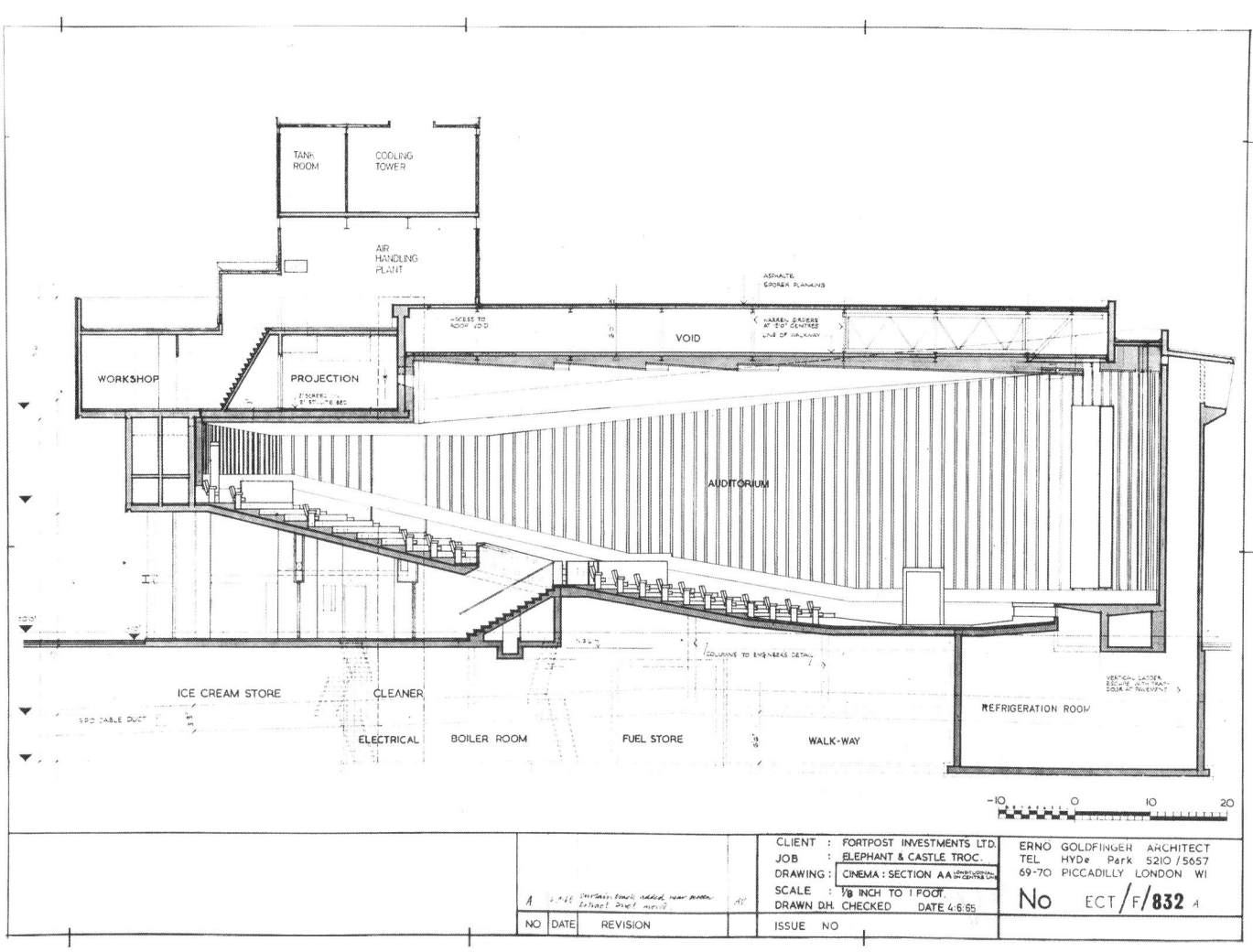

TANK ROOM

COOLING TOWER

AIR HANDLING PLANT

WORKSHOP

PROJECTION

VOID

AUDITORIUM

ICE CREAM STORE

CLEANER

REFRIGERATION ROOM

ELECTRICAL   BOILER ROOM   FUEL STORE   WALK-WAY

CLIENT : FORTPOST INVESTMENTS LTD.
JOB : ELEPHANT & CASTLE TROC.
DRAWING : CINEMA : SECTION AA
SCALE : ⅛ INCH TO 1 FOOT.
DRAWN D.H. CHECKED   DATE 4:6:65

ERNO GOLDFINGER ARCHITECT
TEL HYDe Park 5210 / 5657
69-70 PICCADILLY LONDON WI

No ECT/F/832 A

NO | DATE | REVISION
ISSUE NO

70. Working drawing for Odeon, Elephant and Castle, London, for Fortpost Investments Ltd and Rank Organisation Theatre Division, 1965
Print (375 × 510)

The auditorium was of a conventional stadium type with seating for 1,044 people arranged on a single raked floor – only a third of the capacity of Coles's Trocadero. The sight-lines were carefully worked out with the aid of a wooden model now in the RIBA collection. The main feature of the interior was one of the first uses in this country of the proscenium-free screen or 'flying screen' as it was dubbed because it appeared to float in space with no visible means of support. As the screen lacked proscenium curtains it was filled during intervals with changing abstract patterns of coloured lights – an innovation much in keeping with the sixties' vogue for psychedelic effects. And no, the cinema did not open with a Bond film but with a Cliff Richard vehicle, *Finders Keepers*.

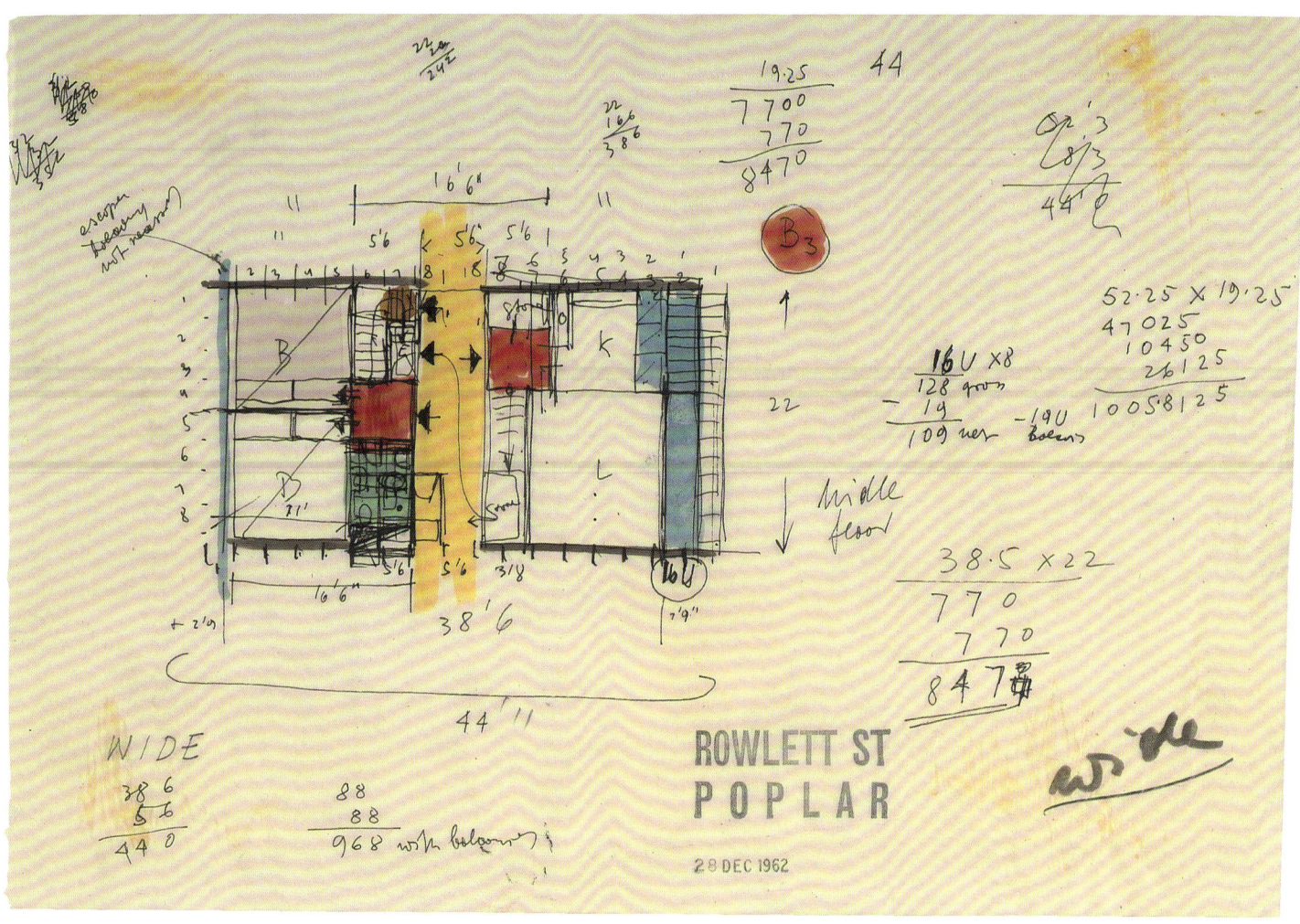

71. Preliminary study for flat layout, Rowlett Street housing, Poplar, London, for the Greater London Council, 1962

Pen and coloured washes on tracing paper (250 × 370)

Goldfinger was finally given the opportunity to realise his ideas on high building in a development for the Greater London Council. This study for flat layouts gives a good insight into his meticulous working methods showing his use in this instance of a 16-foot 6-inch grid, six times his standard grid of 2 feet 9 inches. 'Architecture', wrote Goldfinger, 'is the marriage of the scale of man to the scale of a building.'

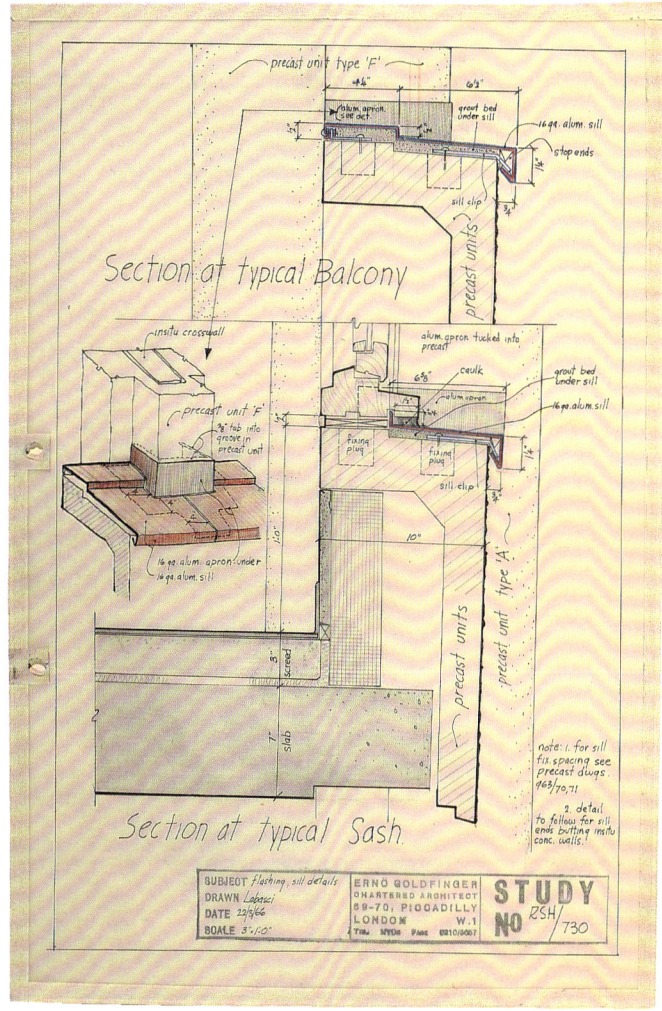

72. Working drawing of sill details, Rowlett Street housing, Poplar, London, for the Greater London Council, 1966

Drawn by Peter Lebasci. Pen, pencil and red and blue crayon on tracing paper (375 × 250)

Goldfinger's designs were always well worked out down to the smallest details and the block, unlike many other high-rise examples, was built to very high technical standards – standards which with the experience gained here were improved at Edenham Street.

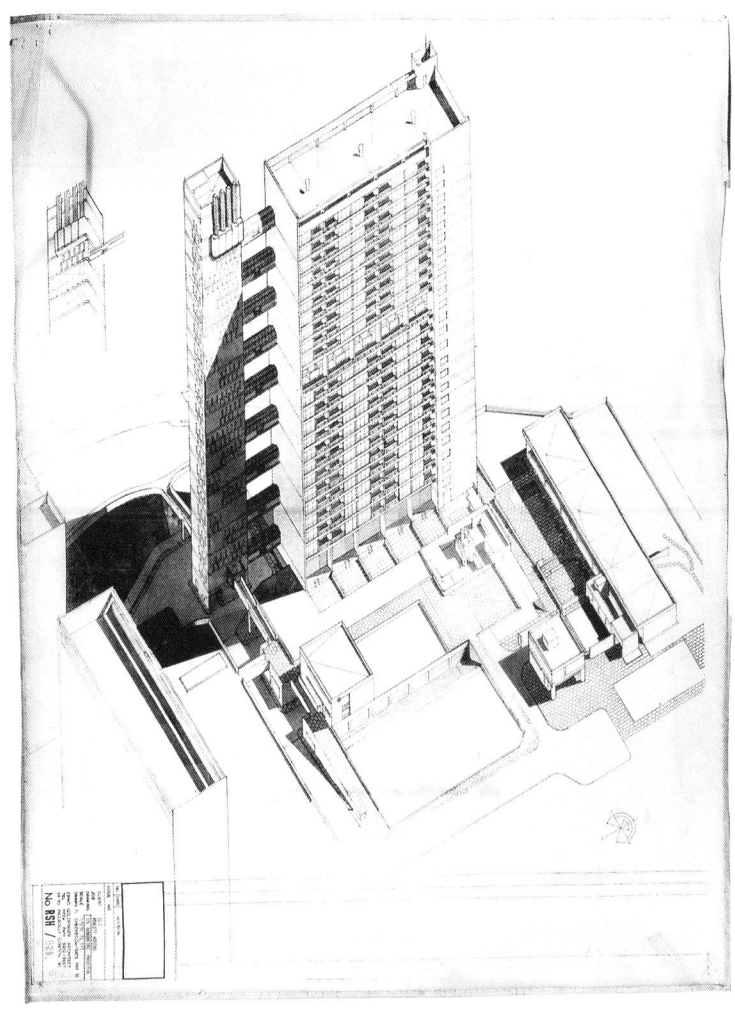

73. Design for Rowlett Street housing, Poplar, London, for the Greater London Council, 1966

Drawn by Peter Lebasci. Print (1040 × 775)

Rowlett Street was built in three phases between 1964 and 1972 and its centrepiece was the 27-storey Balfron Tower, one of the tallest blocks in Europe. As with the Abbots Langley scheme a separate service tower housed the lifts and other noisy machinery well away from the residents and was linked to the main block by a series of access galleries. This concrete tower with its slit windows conjured up a fortress-like air which many found intimidating. Goldfinger's decision to live on the top floor for three months to test how his design worked in practice ensured widespread press coverage but aroused suspicion that what to some seemed a brave sociological experiment was little more than a cheap publicity stunt. Even by the end of his first week's residence Goldfinger felt able to declare himself well satisfied, asserting that 'tall blocks with open spaces were the ideal of the moment. I have wanted to build this for 30 years . . . It will help bring the countryside to London.' The 'thirty years' comment was a reference to his CIAM housing project of 1933, many of the ideas for which Balfron Tower incorporated.

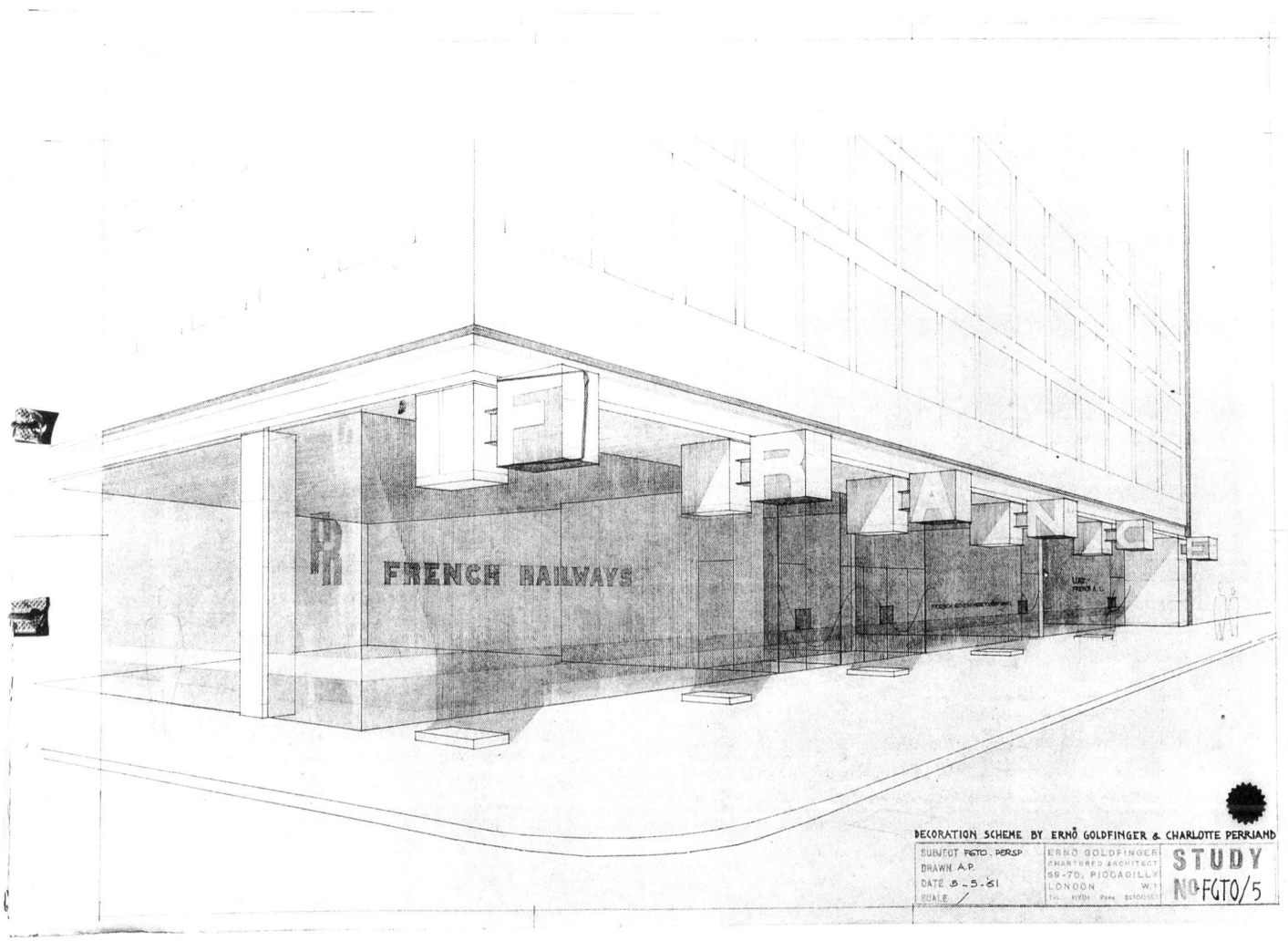

Decoration scheme by Ernö Goldfinger & Charlotte Perriand
SUBJECT FGTO. PERSP
DRAWN A.P.
DATE 8.5.61
SCALE
ERNÖ GOLDFINGER
CHARTERED ARCHITECT
69-70, PICCADILLY
LONDON   W.1
STUDY
No FGTO/5

74. Design for the French Government Tourist Office and SNCF office, Piccadilly, London, 1961

Drawn by Alberto Ponis. Print (380 × 560)

Goldfinger had designed an earlier shop for the French Government Tourist Office in the Haymarket (now destroyed). This commission was for one of a number of offices connected with French travel organisations which were designed by various architects but grouped into a single building. Goldfinger was also responsible for the shop fronts and for this arcade with its polished granite columns and its distinctive illuminated letters, FRANCE. As these were set in wedge-shaped supports at an angle to the facade they could be read up and down Piccadilly – a device which Goldfinger also used at the Odeon, Elephant and Castle.

75. Design for Teesdale, Westwood Road, Windlesham, Surrey, for Mr and Mrs J Perry, 1965

Drawn by WF Pollock. Pencil on tracing paper (760 × 1380)

The Perry house had a difficult gestation and Goldfinger prepared a number of different designs including this early one which is not dissimilar in outline to Frank Lloyd Wright's Mayan block houses. The relationship between architect and client also proved stormy with Jack Perry writing to Goldfinger at one stage: 'You have told me Miss Molis [Goldfinger's assistant] loves the old dining room proportions – (and I want to please Miss Molis). I know you want to retain all the existing proportions – (and I want to please you). I know you are concerned with the aesthetics of form – (and I want to please you), in fact, I am a very pleasant fellow and I want to please everybody including your draughtsman, telephonist, the contractors, the neighbours, the editor of House & Garden, the BBC and Mrs Mary Whitehouse. But may I also please my wife.'

76. Design for Teesdale, Westwood Road, Windlesham, Surrey, for Mr and Mrs J Perry, 1977

Pen, pencil and coloured crayon on tracing paper (575 × 1195)

The final design of cruciform laminated timber posts and laminated timber beams could also be said to recall the work of Frank Lloyd Wright, but this time that of his Usonian period and in particular the Jacobs House at Madison, Wisconsin (1936). Approached by a winding drive the house was carefully situated to take maximum advantage of its densely wooded site which afforded spectacular views of the Surrey countryside. As in the *Ideal Home* bungalow of 1941, day and night usage were separated, this time in two distinct wings linked by a conservatory. One of his last executed works, the Perry house represented an unusual but successful exercise in organic architecture.

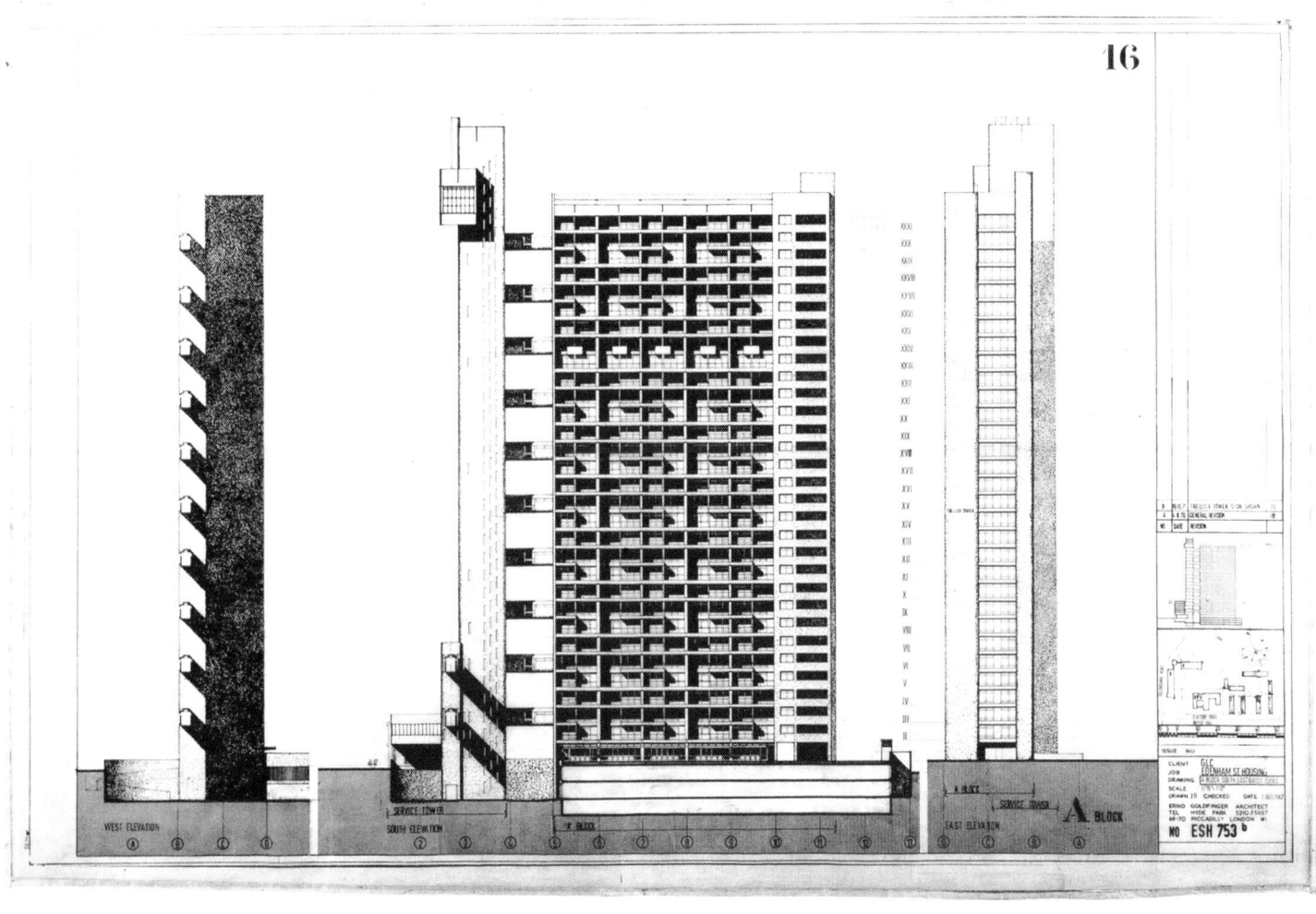

77. Contract drawing for Edenham Street housing, North Kensington, London, for the Greater London Council, 1967

Drawn by John Bains. Pen on tracing paper (710 × 1065)

Overlapping with the Rowlett Street development, but unlike its predecessor conceived as a whole, the Edenham Street estate was built on the site of decaying Victorian terraces close to the Grand Union Canal. The estate, which consisted of a combination of dwellings of varying heights, was again dominated by a massive central block with detached service tower. At thirty-one storeys Trellick Tower was four storeys higher than its forbear and with its slender, sentinel-like service block topped by a boldly cantilevered boiler house it provides one of the most brutally dramatic silhouettes in post-war British architecture. This aggressive mien is highlighted by the bush-hammering of the external concrete, which Goldfinger reckoned produced 'a texture like the Pyramids', and by the slit windows. Unlike Rowlett Street, but consistent with Goldfinger's CIAM housing scheme of 1933, the estate was designed to be an integrated living unit with nursery school, old people's club, shops, hobby rooms, laundry, doctor's surgery and even a pub (though in the end this was never built). Begun in 1966, by the time of its completion in 1972, Edenham Street was an anachronism, residential high-rise having fallen into political, social and architectural disrepute.

78. Design for dwelling types, Edenham Street housing, North Kensington, London, for the Greater London Council, 1976

Drawn by N Omi. Pen and pencil on tracing paper (810 × 1325)

The estate comprised nine main dwelling types and some minor variants. These ranged from two-room flats for the elderly and young couples to five-room, three-storey houses. All were generously planned, with many exceeding the minimum areas laid down in the Parker Morris report. The large balconies, which in Trellick Tower all faced south-west to catch as much sun as possible, the ample bay frontages and the provision of some double height living rooms all added to the general air of spaciousness. This, together with the use of rich colours and more lavish materials than usual in this kind of development, including marble in the entrance hall, helps to account for the estate's general popularity with residents, one long-standing tenant appreciatively remarking, 'Goldfinger thought of everything'.

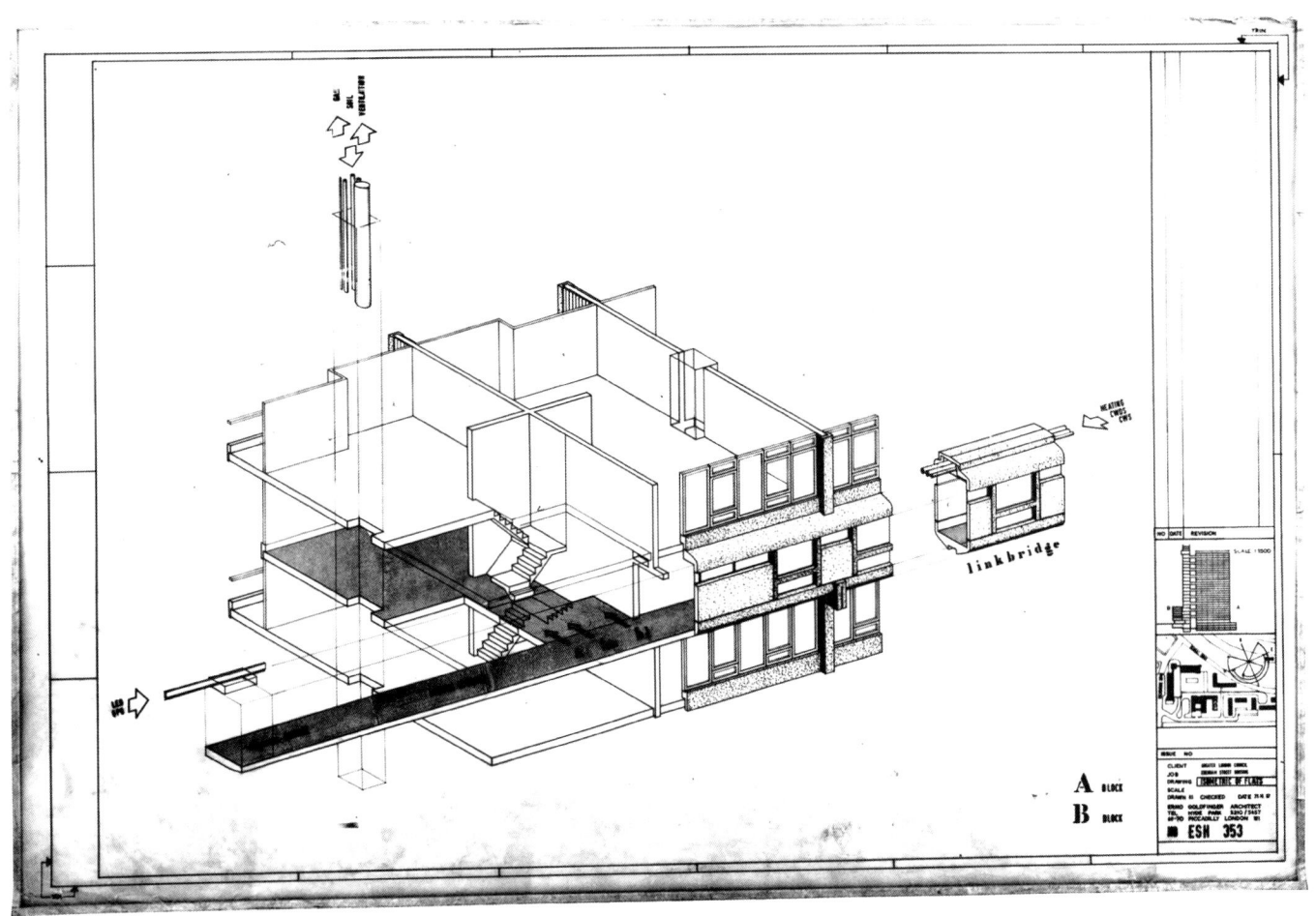

79. Design for Edenham Street housing, North Kensington, London, for the Greater London Council, 1967

Drawn by Robert Sigrist. Pen with mechanical tone on tracing paper (705 × 1070)

Access to the dwellings in Trellick Tower was via the richly embellished entrance hall at the foot of the service tower and thence by lift which, reflecting the planning of the living units, stopped at every third floor.

From there precast concrete link bridges opened on to the access galleries of the residential block. These bridges were cushioned on neoprene pads to prevent noise being transmitted from the service tower.

80. Drawing of the French Government Tourist Office and SNCF office, 127 Avenue des Champs-Elysées, Paris, 1967

Drawn by Juliet Leong. Print with mixed media and collage with overlay with pen, gold paint and collage added (665 × 1035)

In this, the last of the series of buildings which Goldfinger designed for the French Government Tourist Office, his role was restricted to remodelling the structure and facade. The most notable feature of the design was the use for the first time in France of slender water-filled external steel columns which occupied only one-fifth of the space taken up by the previous masonry piers. The executive architect was Pierre Forestier, a former colleague of Goldfinger in the Atelier Perret.

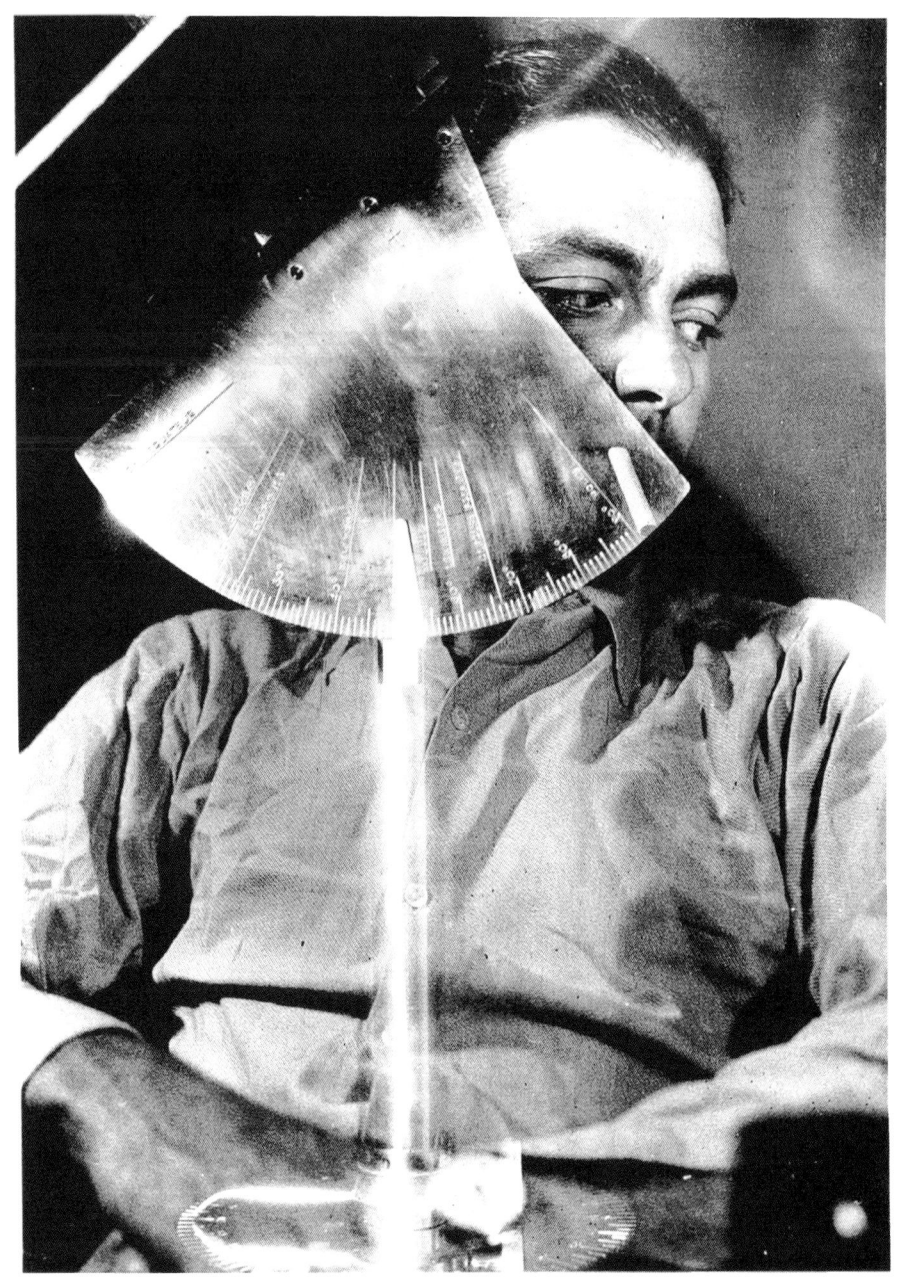

Ernö Goldfinger with his heliometer (photo: Studio Ylla, c 1933)

SELECT BIBLIOGRAPHY

PRIMARY SOURCES

The main primary source is the archive of drawings and manuscripts in the British Architectural Library, RIBA. Goldfinger's photographic archive is now on indefinite loan to the National Trust.

SECONDARY SOURCES
By Ernö Goldfinger

Books

County of London Plan Explained, with EJ Carter, Penguin (London), 1945

British Furniture Today, Tiranti (London), 1951

'The Growth of London', in Sam Lambert (ed), *New Architecture of London*, British Travel & Holidays Association with Architectural Association (London), 1963

'The Sensation of Space', in Dennis Sharp (ed), *Planning and Architecture: Essays Presented to Arthur Korn by the Architectural Association*, Barrie & Rockliff (London), 1967

Periodicals

Ernö Goldfinger contributed regularly to European and American newspapers and journals, including:

'Der neue Baustil' [1925 Exposition, Paris], *Pester Lloyd*, 8 August 1925, p8

'Der Baumeister unserer lieben Frau' [Perret's Notre-Dame, Le Raincy], *Pester Lloyd*, 30 December 1925, p8

'Meubles', with A Szivessy, *L'Organisation ménagère*, June 1928, October 1928

'L'Insolomètre photométrique', *L'Architecture d'aujourd'hui*, vol 5, March 1934, pp[6-7] between pp96, 97

'Une exposition d'architecture à Londres' [MARS Group Exhibition], *L'Architecture d'aujourd'hui*, vol 9, July 1938, pp83-84

'L'exposition de Glasgow 1938', *L'Architecture d'aujourd'hui*, vol 9, October 1938, pp27-29

'Living in Cities', *Horizon*, June 1941

'Planning for the Future: 9. This Easy-to-Run One-Floor Home', with Mary Crowley, *Ideal Home*, vol 44, October 1941, pp174-77

'The Sensation of Space', *The Architectural Review*, vol 90, November 1941, pp129-31

'Urbanism and Spatial Order', *The Architectural Review*, vol 90, December 1941, pp163-66

'The Elements of Enclosed Space', *The Architectural Review*, vol 91, January 1942, pp5-8

'Producer Control and Consumer Control', *Architect & Building News*, vol 169, 16 January 1942, pp64-65

'Town and Country Planning Association's Conference at Cambridge', *Architects' Journal*, vol 95, 23 April 1942, pp300-03

'Planning for the Future: 19. For the Family: a House, a Flat . . . or Something Between the Two?', *Ideal Home*, vol 46, September 1942, pp128-31

'The Voice of the Industry' [Standardisation], *Architect & Building News*, vol 173, 15 January 1943, p54

'Staatliche Bauforschung', *Werk*, vol 34, April 1947, pp119-20

'L'Organisation de la santé publique en Angleterre', *L'Architecture d'aujourd'hui*, vol 18, November 1947, pp14-15

'Le centre de santé. Le rôle du centre de santé dans le plan anglais', *L'Architecture d'aujourd'hui*, vol 18, November 1947, pp20-21

'Dinner for Six' [one of contributors], *Building*, vol 24, January 1949, pp24-28; February 1949, pp49-52; March 1949, pp102-04

'Architecture – the Art of Enclosing Space', *Architectural Association Journal*, vol 63, March 1948, pp177-87

'Moore and Matisse', *Building*, vol 23, December 1948, pp386-87

'Le problème du logement en Grande-Bretagne', *L'Architecture d'aujourd'hui*, vol 20, September 1950, p19

'L'architecture contemporaine en Grande-Bretagne', *L'Architecture d'aujourd'hui*, vol 22, February 1952, p3

'Characteristics and Requirements of Patent Glazing', *Architectural Design*, vol 24, March 1954, pp137-42

'Auguste Perret', *The Architectural Review*, vol 115, May 1954, p341

'Focus on France' special issue (guest editor), *Architectural Design*, vol 24, July 1954

'The Work of Auguste Perret', *Architectural Association Journal*, vol 70, January 1955, pp144-56

'The Work of Auguste Perret', *American Institute of Architects. Journal*, vol 23, May 1955, pp195-200 and June 1955, pp273-76

'Londres', *L'Architecture d'aujourd'hui*, vol 26, December 1955, p37

'Auguste Perret, 1874-1954', *Architects' Year Book*, vol 7, 1956, pp43-53

'"Das Haus auf der Insel", Hier Spricht London' (BBC broadcast), 11 May 1957

'André Sive', *The Times*, 25 September 1958, p15

'History [of London]', *Architectural Design*, vol 31, June 1961, pp235-39

'Elephant & Castle – Site II', *Architectural Association Journal*, vol 77, April 1962, pp244-49

'Analyse critique de certains termes propres aux urbanistes britanniques', *L'Architecture d'aujourd'hui*, vol 35, December/February 1964/65, pp56-59

'Cosmorama. Vers une Architecture' [obituary of Le Corbusier], *Architectural Design*, vol 35, October 1965, pp474, 476

'L'Habitat en Grande Bretagne', *L'Architecture d'aujourd'hui*, vol 38, February/March 1967, pp42-45

'Hommages [Victor Bourgeois]', *La Maison*, vol 23, December 1967, p6
'Balfron Tower', *East London Papers*, Summer 1969
'Le Corbusier at Pessac', *RIBA Journal*, vol 76, September 1969, pp381-82
'[Auguste Perret] The Last of the Master Builders', *Building Design*, no. 240, 7 March 1975, pp14-15
'Chermayeff: Ahead of his Time', *Architects' Journal*, vol 172, 15 October 1980, p738
'A Meeting of Minds: To Mark the 50th Anniversary of the CIAM Congress that Produced the Athens Charter', with James Dunnett, *Architects' Journal*, vol 178, 14 December 1983, pp26-30

ON GOLDFINGER

Books

Dunnett, James, and Gavin Stamp, *Works I: Ernö Goldfinger*, Architectural Association (London), 1983
Ginsburger, Roger, *Junge französische Architekten*, Meister der Baukunst (Geneva), 1930
Major, Máté, *Goldfinger Ernö*, Akadémiai Kiadó (Budapest), 1973

Periodicals

Benton, Charlotte, 'The Importance of Being Ernö', *Building Design*, no. 642, 27 May 1983, pp24-25
Cadbury-Brown, HT, 'Goldfinger', *Architects' Journal*, vol 157, 31 January 1973, pp240-42
Cadbury-Brown, HT, John Winter and James Dunnett, 'Ernö Goldfinger: a Tribute', *RIBA Transactions*, no. 2, 1982, pp19-26
Chester, Lewis, 'High and Mighty', *The Guardian Weekend*, 16 July 1994, pp28-30
Dunnett, James, 'Ernö Goldfinger: the Architect as Constructor', *The Architectural Review*, vol 173, April 1983, pp42-46
'Ernö Goldfinger Talks to the Architectural Review', *The Architectural Review*, vol 173, April 1983, pp47-48
Hofer, Miklos, 'Goldfinger Ernö', Magyar Epítömüvészet, vol 83, no. 6, 1992, p53
Lowrie, Joyce, 'The Work of Ernö Goldfinger' special issue, *Architectural Design*, vol 33, January 1963
McNay, Michael, 'Goldfinger Points Upwards', *The Guardian*, 8 March 1969
Rawsthorne, Peter, 'Buildings Scaled to People', *Sunday Telegraph*, 3 June 1962
Richards, JM, 'Pleasure offered to the eye: Ernö Goldfinger', *AA Files*, no. 5, January 1984, pp94-99
Stamp, Gavin, 'Conversation with Ernö Goldfinger', *Thirties Society Journal*, no. 2, 1982, pp19-24
Stamp, Gavin, 'Goldfinger: the Original', *The Spectator*, 11 June 1983, pp30-31
Waroff, Deborah, 'Goldfinger', *Building Design*, no. 199, 3 May 1974, p6
Winter, John, 'Goldfinger at 80', *Architects' Journal*, vol 176, 15 September 1982, pp52-54

Wislocki, Peter and Bronagh Carey, 'Working with the Masters' [John Winter on Ernö Goldfinger], *Architects' Journal*, vol 192, 19/26 December 1990, p44

Obituaries

Abram, Joseph, 'Ernö Goldfinger: 1902-1987', *L'Architecture d'aujourd'hui*, vol 59, April 1988, pp061-062
Benton, Charlotte, 'Classic Modernist: Ernö Goldfinger 1902-1987', *Building Design*, no. 862, 20 November 1987, p10
Cadbury-Brown, HT, 'Ernö Goldfinger', *The Architectural Review*, vol 183, January 1988, pp4-5
Dunnett, James, 'Ernö Goldfinger', *Architects' Journal*, vol 186, 25 November 1987, pp28-29
'Ernö Goldfinger', *Daily Telegraph*, 16 November 1987
'Ernö Goldfinger', *Building*, vol 252, 27 November 1987, p15
'Golden Touch', *The Guardian*, 18 November 1987, p27
Hofer, Miklos, 'Goldfinger Ernö 1902-1987', *Magyar Epítömüvészet*, vol 79, no. 3, 1988, pp53-55
'Mr Ernö Goldfinger', *The Times*, 16 November 1987
Winter, John, 'Ernö Goldfinger', *RIBA Journal*, vol 95, February 1988, p90

PRINCIPAL REFERENCES TO THE BUILDINGS ILLUSTRATED

Design for a lantern tower
Ecole Nationale Supérieure des Beaux-Arts. Concours d'architecture, vol 16, 1924/25, pp3-4

Design for an architect's office
Ecole Nationale Supérieure des Beaux-Arts. Concours d'architecture, vol 17, 1925/26, p12

Design for law courts
Ecole Nationale Supérieure des Beaux-Arts. Concours d'architecture, vol 16, 1924/25, pp8-9

Design for metal chair with sprung seat
Ginsburger, Roger, *Junge französische Architekten*, Meister der Baukunst (Geneva), 1930, p114
Architectural Design, vol 33, January 1963, p44

Design for a railway terminus clock
Ecole Nationale Supérieure des Beaux-Arts. Concours d'architecture, vol 18, 1926/27, p14

Design for a shooting club
Ecole Nationale Supérieure des Beaux-Arts. Concours d'architecture, vol 17, 1925/26, p17
Architectural Design, vol 33, January 1963, p10

Design for a reservoir
Ecole Nationale Supérieure des Beaux-Arts. Concours d'architecture, vol 18, 1926/27, pp11-12
Architectural Design, vol 33, January 1963, p10

Design for a commemorative chapel
Ecole Nationale Supérieure des Beaux-Arts. Concours d'architecture vol 17, 1925/26, p18

Palace of Justice, San Salvador
Architectural Design, vol 33, January 1963, p12

Helena Rubinstein salon, Grafton Street, London
Poulain, Roger, *Boutiques*, Vincent Freal (Paris), 1929, plates 54-56
Ginsburger, Roger, *Junge französische Architekten*, Meister der Baukunst (Geneva), 1930, pp90-91
The Architectural Review, vol 78, July 1935, pp26-27
Architects' Journal, vol 84, 10 December 1936, p815
Architects' Journal, vol 85, 18 March 1937, p479
Westwood, Bryan and Norman, *Smaller Retail Shops*, Architectural Press (London), 1937, pp16, 72
Westwood, Bryan and Norman, *The Modern Shop*, Architectural Press (London), 1952, pp35, 127
Architectural Design, vol 33, January 1963, p11

Furniture designs
Lever, Jill, *Architects' Designs for Furniture*, Trefoil (London), 1982, pp128-29

Skikda Palace Hotel, Philippeville, Algeria
Poulain, Roger, *Batiments: civils, industriels, commerciaux*, Vincent Freal (Paris), 1930, plates 18-20
Ginsburger, Roger, *Junge französische Architekten*, Meister der Baukunst (Geneva), 1930, pp50-54
Architectural Design, vol 33, January 1963, p12

Design for a flying club
Architectural Design, vol 33, January 1963, p13

Heliometer
L'Architecture d'aujourd'hui, vol 5, March 1934, pp[6-7] between pp96, 97
Architectural Design, vol 33, January 1963, pp53-54

CIAM housing project
Architectural Design, vol 33, January 1963, p14
Architects' Journal, vol 178, 14 December 1983, pp26-30

The Outlook, Le Touquet
Decorative Art, vol 33, 1938, p77
Decorative Art, vol 34, 1939, p30
Hastings, Alan (ed), *Week-end Houses, Cottages and Bungalows*, Architectural Press (London), 1939, pp88-90
Architectural Design, vol 33, January 1963, pp15-16
Lever, Jill, *Architects' Designs for Furniture*, Trefoil (London), 1982, pp129, 130

Children's nesting chair
Lever, Jill, *Architects' Designs for Furniture*, Trefoil (London), 1982, pp129, 130

Waterfield house, Broxted, Essex
Hastings, Alan (ed), *Week-end Houses, Cottages and Bungalows*, Architectural Press (London), 1939, pp106-07
Yorke, FRS, *Modern Houses in England*, Architectural Press (Cheam), 1944, pp56-57
Architectural Association Journal, vol 63, March 1948, pp181-82
L'Architecture d'aujourd'hui, vol 30, March 1950, p30
La Maison, vol 9, November 1953, p353
Architectural Design, vol 33, January 1963, p19
Country Life, vol 184, 8 February 1990, p92

S Weiss shop, 2 Golders Green Road, London
Architects' Journal, vol 83, 18 June 1936, pp439-40
The Architectural Review, vol 79, June 1936, p272
The Architectural Review, vol 80, August 1936 supplement, pp83-96
Architectural Design, vol 33, January 1963, p17

Abbatt shop, 94 Wimpole Street, London
The Architectural Review, vol 81, January 1937, pp24-25
Architects' Journal, vol 85, 11 February 1937, p277
Architects' Journal, vol 86, 2 September 1937, pp371-72
Westwood, Bryan and Norman, *Smaller Retail Shops*, Architectural Press (London), 1937, p96
Architectural Design, vol 33, January 1963, p18

Easiwork furniture
The Architectural Review, vol 82, December 1937, pp291-93
Architectural Design, vol 33, January 1963, p50

ICI stand, 1938 British Industries Fair, London
Architects' Journal, vol 87, 24 February 1938, p316

1-3 Willow Road, Hampstead, London
The Architectural Review, vol 87, April 1940, pp126-30 and supplement, pp149-53
Architects' Journal, vol 91, 25 April 1940, pp427-30
Architect & Building News, vol 162, 28 June 1940, pp242-47
Yorke, FRS, *Modern Houses in England*, Architectural Press (Cheam), 1944, pp94-96
Architectural Association Journal, vol 63, March 1948, p181
L'Architecture d'aujourd'hui, vol 19, July 1948, pp67-68
La Maison, vol 9, November 1953, pp348-50
House and Garden, vol 10, October 1955, pp86-89
Architectural Design, vol 33, January 1963, pp20-23
Country Life, vol 185, 12 September 1991, pp146-49
Apollo, vol 141, April 1995, pp45-49

Nursery school
Builder, vol 158, 12 April 1940, p436

Ideal Home bungalow
Ideal Home, vol 44, October 1941, pp174-77

Holiday and evacuation camp
Architect & Building News, vol 160, 27 October 1939, pp88-89
Builder, vol 157, 27 October 1939, pp615-16
Architect & Building News, vol 160, 10 November 1939, pp138-40
Keystone, March 1940
Architect & Building News, vol 161, 8 March 1940, p239
Architects' Journal, vol 91, 21 March 1940, p295
Architect & Building News, vol 161, 22 March 1940, pp288-89

Box-frame housing
Arup, Ove, *Safe Housing in Wartime*, 1941
Arup, Ove, *Memorandum on Box Frame Construction for Terrace Houses and Flats*, 1944

Typical modern type of urban enclosure
The Architectural Review, vol 91, January 1942, p8
Ideal Home, vol 46, September 1942, pp128-31

ABT prefabricated housing
Cox, Bernard H, *Prefabricated Homes*, Paul Elek (London), 1945

Daily Worker, Farringdon Road, London
The Architectural Review, vol 106, August 1949, pp101-04
Architects' Journal, vol 111, 19 January 1950, p88
Building, vol 25, March 1950, pp106-13
Architects' Journal, vol 187, 7 September 1988, p6

Prefabricated construction system for schools
L'Architecture d'aujourd'hui, no. 25, August/September 1949, pp46-47
Architects' Journal, vol 113, 14 June 1951, pp768-72
Architectural Design, vol 22, July 1952, pp184-93
The Architectural Review, vol 112, July 1952, pp30-37
Architect & Building News, vol 202, 31 July 1952, pp137-46
Techniques et architecture, vol 12, April 1953, pp86-91
Architectural Design, vol 33, January 1963, p24

10 Regent's Park Road, London
Architectural Design, vol 24, April 1954, p105
House and Garden, vol 11, August 1956, pp30-33
Architectural Design, vol 26, September 1956, pp280-82
Architectural Design, vol 31, June 1961, p262
Ideal Home, vol 86, November 1962, pp121-30
Architectural Design, vol 33, January 1963, pp25-26

Carr & Co, Birmingham
L'Architecture d'aujourd'hui, vol 26, September 1955, pXXV
The Architectural Review, vol 119, January 1956, pp50, 53

The Architectural Review, vol 124, September 1958, pp153-59
Architectural Design, vol 28, October 1958, pp394-99
L'Architecture d'aujourd'hui, vol 30, February/March 1959, pp58-60
Manasseh, Leonard and Roger Cunliffe, *Office Buildings*, Batsford (London), 1962, pp166-69
Architectural Design, vol 33, January 1963, pp29-30

45-46 Albemarle Street, London
Architectural Design, vol 25, October 1955, p313
The Architectural Review, vol 119, January 1956, pp39-40
The Architectural Review, vol 120, October 1956, p225
Architects' Journal, vol 126, 18 July 1957, pp105-07
Architects' Journal, vol 126, 25 July 1957, pp133-34
New Yorker, 28 September 1957, p118
Architects' Journal, vol 127, 16 January 1958, pp98-99
Architectural Design, vol 28, January 1958, pp1-6
The Architectural Review, vol 123, February 1958, pp118-23
New Statesman, 26 April 1958, p529
Architecture & Building, vol 33, October 1958, pp374-83
L'Architecture d'aujourd'hui, vol 30, February/March 1959, pp60-61
Dannatt, Trevor, *Modern Architecture in Britain*, Batsford (London), 1959, pp59-62
Architectural Design, vol 31, June 1961, p284
Manasseh, Leonard and Roger Cunliffe, *Office Buildings*, Batsford (London), 1962, pp125-29
Architectural Design, vol 33, January 1963, pp27-28
Architects' Journal, vol 192, 7 November 1990, pp6-7
Architects' Journal, vol 193, 1 May 1991, p11

Office skyscraper, Moorgate, London
Architects' Journal, vol 121, 23 June 1955, pp846-48
Architectural Design, vol 25, June 1955, pp178-81
Techniques et architecture, vol 15, September 1955, pp10-13
Architectural Design, vol 33, January 1963, p41

Housing, Hunton Bridge Road, Abbots Langley
The Architectural Review, vol 127, January 1960, p59
The Architectural Review, vol 129, May 1961, pp344-46
Baumeister, vol 61, December 1964, pp1392-94
L'Architecture d'aujourd'hui, vol 35, April/May, p43

This Is Tomorrow exhibition, Whitechapel Art Gallery, London
The Times, 9 August 1956
The Spectator, 17 August 1956, p234

House in the Vale of Health, Hampstead, London
Architects' Journal, vol 128, 6 November 1958, p661
Architect & Building News, vol 214, 19 November 1958, pp665, 669-70
Architects' Journal, vol 128, 20 November 1958, p733
Architects' Journal, vol 128, 4 December 1958, pp806-07
Architects' Journal, vol 129, 12 March 1959, p399
Architectural Design, vol 33, January 1963, p41

Office building, 69-70 Piccadilly, London
The Architectural Review, vol 123, January 1958, p41
Architecture & Building, vol 33, October 1958, p383
Architectural Design, vol 33, January 1963, p41

Hille House, Watford
The Architectural Review, vol 125, January 1959, pp58-59
Architects' Journal, vol 130, 27 August 1959, p81
The Guardian, 3 March 1961, p24
Architects' Journal, vol 133, 16 March 1961, p411
Interior Design, July/August 1961, pp222-23
The Architectural Review, vol 130, August 1961, pp84-87
Architectural Design, vol 33, January 1963, pp31-32

Alexander Fleming House, Elephant and Castle, London
Architectural Design, vol 29, October 1959, p420
The Architectural Review, vol 127, January 1960, pp40-43
L'Architecture d'aujourd'hui, vol 31, February/March 1960, p29
Architects' Journal, vol 135, 7 March 1962, p506
Architectural Association Journal, vol 77, April 1962, pp244-49
Civil Engineer, April 1962, pp167-68
Architectural Design, vol 33, January 1963, pp38-40
The Guardian, 3 January 1963
The Architectural Review, vol 133, February 1963, pp94-101
L'Architecture d'aujourd'hui, vol 34, December/January 1963/64, pp16-17
Baumeister, vol 61, May 1964, pp496-97
Architecture formes et fonctions, vol 13, 1967, pp163-67
The Architectural Review, vol 141, April 1967, pp280-85
Architectural Design, vol 37, October 1967, pp447-52
L'Architecture d'aujourd'hui, vol 38, December/January 1967/68, pp72-75
La Maison, vol 24, April 1968, pp161-62
Architects' Journal, vol 188, 22 June 1988, p6
Building Design, no. 896, 29 July 1988, pp1, 2
Casabella, vol 52, November 1988, p33
Building Design, no. 913, 2 December 1988, p11
Architects' Journal, vol 189, 14 June 1989, pp26-33
Building Design, no. 941, 16 June 1989, p5
Architects' Journal, vol 190, 9 August 1989, pp26-27
Building Design, no. 1030, 12 April 1991, pp1, 2

Shopping Centre, Elephant and Castle, London
Architects' Journal, vol 132, 21 July 1960, pp103-04
Architect & Building News, vol 218, 27 July 1960, pp112-13
Architectural Design, vol 33, January 1963, p42

Lime Tree House, Combe Hill Road, Malden
Architectural Design, vol 33, January 1963, pp34-37
Baumeister, vol 61, December 1964, pp1400-01
Building Design, no. 1191, 23 September 1994, p1
Building Design, no. 1203, 13 January 1995, p4

Bloomsbury Square development project, London
Architect & Building News, vol 223, 20 February 1963, p262

Odeon, Elephant and Castle, London
Architects' Journal, vol 139, 6 May 1964, p1065
Architect & Building News, vol 225, 13 May 1964, pp849-50
Builder, vol 206, 15 May 1964, p1014
The Architectural Review, vol 139, January 1966, p67
Architects' Journal, vol 144, 27 July 1966, p213
Architecture formes et fonctions, vol 13, 1967, pp163-67
New Society, 26 January 1967, p135
The Architectural Review, vol 141, April 1967, pp286-88
Architects' Journal, vol 145, 19 April 1967, pp949, 959
Architectural Design, vol 37, October 1967, pp446-52
L'Architecture d'aujourd'hui, vol 38, December/January 1967/68, p75
Architects' Journal, vol 150, 17 September 1969, pp709-22
Building Design, no. 899, 19 August 1988, p5
Architects' Journal, vol 187, 24/31 August 1988, p6

Rowlett Street housing, Poplar, London
L'Architecture d'aujourd'hui, vol 38, February/March 1967, pp50-51
East London Papers, Summer 1969

French Government Tourist Office and SNCF office, Piccadilly, London
The Architectural Review, vol 134, September 1963, pp183-84
Architectural Design, vol 33, December 1963, pp601-03
Architect & Building News, vol 225, 4 March 1964, detail sheet 774
Architect & Building News, vol 225, 11 March 1964, detail sheet 775

Teesdale, Westwood Road, Windlesham
Architectural Design, vol 40, August 1970, pp418-19
House and Garden, vol 25, September 1970, pp48-51
L'Architecture d'aujourd'hui, vol 44, August/September 1972, pp24-25
A + U, vol 3, December 1973, pp66-69

Edenham Street housing, North Kensington, London
The Architectural Review, vol 143, January 1968, p72
Building Design, no. 54, 28 May 1971, p4
Architects' Journal, vol 157, 10 January 1973, pp77-96
Architettura Cronache e Storia, vol 19, May 1973, pp38-39
Architects' Journal, vol 157, 18 April 1973, p901
Ekistics, vol 36, November 1973, pp334-36
Architects' Journal, vol 176, 29 September 1982, p25
Architects' Journal, vol 181, 27 February 1985, p22
Architects' Journal, vol 194, 17 July 1991, p7

French Government Tourist Office and SNCF office, Champs-Elysées, Paris
Building with Steel, no. 15, August 1973, pp31-32

INDEX

(page references in italic indicate illustrations)